593720842799

WITHD[

D0386757

BIG DADDY'S RULES

Raising Daughters Is Tougher Than I Look

STEVE SCHIRRIPA

with Philip Lerman

A TOUCHSTONE BOOK
Published by Simon & Schuster
New York London Toronto Sydney New Delhi

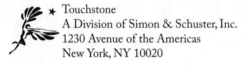 ★ Touchstone
A Division of Simon & Schuster, Inc.
1230 Avenue of the Americas
New York, NY 10020

First Touchstone hardcover edition May 2013

TOUCHSTONE and colophon are registered trademarks of Simon & Schuster, Inc.

For information about special discounts for bulk purchases,
please contact Simon & Schuster Special Sales at 1-866-506-1949
or business@simonandschuster.com.

The Simon & Schuster Speakers Bureau can bring authors to your live event.
For more information or to book an event, contact the Simon & Schuster Speakers
Bureau at 866-248-3049 or visit our website at www.simonspeakers.com.

Designed by Aline C. Pace

Manufactured in the United States of America

10 9 8 7 6 5 4 3 2 1

Library of Congress Cataloging-in-Publication Data

Schirripa, Steven R.
    Big daddy's rules : raising daughters is tougher than I look / by Steve Schirripa with
Philip Lerman.
        pages   cm
    1. Fathers and daughters.   2. Child rearing.   3. Parenting.   I. Title.
    HQ755.85.S35 2013
    306.874'2—dc23   2013005504

ISBN 978-1-4767-0634-4
ISBN 978-1-4767-0636-8 (ebook)

For Laura, Bria, and Ciara,
the loves of my life

Contents

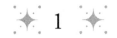

THAT'S *MISTER* DAD TO YOU

Sometimes being a dad is like watching a ping-pong match.

I'm in the dining room the other day, and my wife and one of my girls start up on one of those things mothers and daughters seem to be able to get into with no end in sight:

You're not going out in that skirt. It's too short.

No it isn't.

Yes it is.

But I wore it last week.

I don't care, it's too short.

But Gina is wearing a shorter skirt.

I'm not Gina's mother. I said you can't go out like that.

Back and forth. I try to hold my tongue and let them work it out.

That lasts about no seconds.

I explode, like the firecrackers we used to toss in the garbage cans on Bath Avenue when I was growing up in Brooklyn.

As loud as I can, with my face getting as red as a can of tomato sauce, I make my point clear:

"Did you not hear your mother! Did she not just tell you you're not going out of the house with your ass hanging out the back of your skirt! What part of 'you're not going out of the house with your ass hanging out the back of your skirt' do you not understand?"

They both roll their eyes. They've heard this all before.

I take a little pause for effect—all those acting lessons weren't for nothing, you know—and then I ratchet it up a notch.

"I don't care who else wears what, anywhere else in the world, I don't care whether you think this skirt is appropriate, and I don't care about anything, to be honest, other than when your mother tells you to change your skirt, you change your skirt. Does anyone here have a problem with that?"

At this point, they're looking at each other. It's a bonding moment for the two of them: Oh, well, I guess Dad's at it again.

No one gets upset. No one talks back. They smirk, and they wait for the storm to pass.

And then my daughter goes back into her room and changes her skirt.

Welcome to the world of the Big Daddy.

Listen. Everywhere you look these days, somebody's making fun of dads. You turn on the TV on Father's Day, and they're showing all the daddy movies, and in one after another, the dad is an idiot—he can't make breakfast, he can't make lunch, he can't get piss out of a boot if the instructions are written on the heel. He sure as hell can't change a diaper, dress his kids, or give his teenage daughters advice on anything beyond how to buy car insurance, and even for that he needs help from a fucking gecko that sounds like Keith Richards.

Well, I say, enough is enough.

I'd like to form a club just for fathers. Specifically fathers of daughters. There would be lots of overstuffed leather chairs, wood paneling, dim lights. The works. A good space for sitting around and talking and getting some shit off our chests.

I don't mean all the time, of course. Just during the commercials.

And instead of a THIS BUD'S FOR YOU sign, there would be a burnt-wood sign, hanging over the good Scotch, reading:

WHOEVER SAYS WE DON'T KNOW
WHAT THE FUCK WE'RE TALKING ABOUT
DOESN'T KNOW WHAT THE FUCK THEY'RE TALKING ABOUT

Because all of this talk about what idiots dads are, and how we have to learn to be a pal to our kids, and how we have to learn to be more like moms—I've had it up to here with all of that.

I say it's time for the Big Daddys to take over.

I gotta say, as the father of two beautiful young daughters, I consider myself the luckiest man on the face of the earth. I know for most guys that means you've got Lou Gehrig's disease, but I don't mean it that way. I mean yeah, being the father of girls is a kind of illness, in its own way—since any guy who has tried to live in a house with a wife and two daughters is, without any doubt, going to go certifiably nuts.

But I wouldn't have it any other way.

I play this father, Leo, on a TV show called *The Secret Life of the American Teenager.* He's the father of a nice teenage boy who gets into more trouble than any kid you've ever known (if you're lucky). A girl he knows gets pregnant, he starts dating her and decides he's going to marry her, then he gets another girl pregnant and decides he's gonna marry her instead. And this is a kid who's barely started shaving.

Leo is the owner of a successful meat company. He deals with all of his kid's problems intelligently, calmly but firmly guiding his child through the rough waters of life.

In other words, he's nothing like me.

I will say this from the get-go: When it comes to being a dad, I think staying calm is overrated. I got no patience for a lot of what I see going on around me, with my kids, with other kids, and especially with other parents. And I'm not shy about saying so. Sometimes, very loudly. The occasional dish does get broken in the course of certain discussions. When people tell me that I'm a hothead, I have one response:

You got a problem with that?

Let me give you an example.

A few years back I'm in a restaurant in the Village with my family. It's a nice restaurant; white tablecloths, waiters who are all out-of-work actors waiting for their big break. They don't just tell you what's on the menu, they perform it. (And why is it the more expensive the restaurant, the more they feel they have to tell you every ingredient that went into every dish? "The salmon is braised in a smoked honey-cilantro vinaigrette with thyme, corn nuts, pickled snail tongues, and a hint of dog's breath." Just give me the goddamn dish. I don't have to know its life story. You go into an Italian restaurant, you don't get that. "Would you like the veal pic-cata?" "Can you tell me how it's prepared?" "Yeah, we cook it, then we bring it out to the table." "Sounds good. I'll have that.")

Anyway, so we're at this really nice restaurant, me and the family. My older daughter is about sixteen at the time. The waiter has finally gotten through his performance of "Specials of the Day"— beautiful job, I have to say, his description of the she-crab soup brought us to tears—and we're just settling in, and I notice there's this big-mouth guy sitting across from us. The restaurant's tiny, not much bigger than my living room, and he's talking like he's giving the State of the Union address. Sitting with two other guys, and the big blowhard is going on and on, and he's kind of irritating me, so the manager, who I know, I said to him, "What's up with this guy? Who is this guy?" I said, "Tell him to shut up, because he's disrupting everybody's meal." But the guy doesn't shut up.

So later, I get the check, and my daughter gets up to walk out and passes the guy, and he leans way out of his seat to look at her butt. And he passes a remark to the guy he's sitting with.

Mount Saint Helens didn't erupt so quickly.

"Are you kidding me?" I scream at the guy. "Are you kidding me?"

Now the whole restaurant is quiet. You could hear a pin drop. I can tell I've got the guy's attention because it's the first time he's shut up all night.

"She's sixteen years old," I said. "That's my daughter. She's sixteen years old and you want to look at her ass? Is that what you want to do? You want to look at my daughter's ass? You ruin everybody's goddamn dinner, and now you want to look at my daughter's ass?"

I told him and his two buddies to come outside.

Now, I'm fifty years old at the time, and fat, and these guys are half my age and half my weight, and my wife is telling me to calm down. I told her, go get in the cab, because when they come out I'm gonna fight them, and I'm probably gonna get beat up but I'm gonna fight 'em because that's how mad this guy got me.

My wife and kids just smiled and shrugged. They got in the cab, and the driver flipped the meter, and they sat and waited and started talking about something else. They're used to this with me.

The three guys never came out, and eventually I got in the cab with them, and we headed out.

"Having fun, Dad?" my daughter said to me as the cab pulled away from the curb.

"Just watching out for you, sweetheart," I said.

And I was. The point is, everybody thinks they have the answer to how to be a good parent. Here's mine: Everybody's gonna make mistakes. Kids don't come with an instruction manual. So if you're gonna make mistakes, at least make them your own way.

Me, I don't use the word "parenting." It's not a verb. It's a noun. You're a parent. A mom or a dad. You're not there to be a friend to your kid. I see these moms, they think they can be a friend to their daughters. A woman I know, I kid you not, she and her teenage daughter went off to get tattoos together.

This is not a message you want to give to a teenage kid. If she's gonna get tattoos when her mom is right there, what's she gonna do when you're not around? Kids have to rebel. It's their nature. It's their job. Your job is to give them something to rebel against. What does that kid with the tattoos have to do in order to piss her mother off, shoot somebody? Maybe after the tattoos they can go for a nice mother-daughter manicure, pedicure, and bank robbery.

How to Be a Big Daddy

My kids know that for better or for worse—and sometimes for a little of both—I am going to be Enormously Present. The Big Daddy, in all senses of the word.

For me, it's not enough to stand on the sidelines and watch your wife raise your kids. For me, it's all about getting in the game.

That's Big Daddy rule number one.

Get off the goddamn bench.

Because look. I give my kids a good life. Growing up poor like I did, not knowing where the next meal was coming from, you decide that your kids are never going to go without good food. Growing up with cardboard in your sneakers (when you even had sneakers), you decide that your kids are never going to go without nice shoes. Growing up without anything, you want to give your kids everything. Do I give them too much? Probably. They have a nice life, and I'm happy that they have a nice life.

But I am not above threatening to take it all away. I've said it so many times, they could probably recite it themselves, like Don Corleone's speech in *The Godfather*. I've said—and not, you may guess by now, in the quietest of tones—you like this life? The nice apartment, the nice clothes, the nice vacations, the Knicks tickets, the whole nine yards? You screw up and it all goes away. The first time you come home with liquor on your breath, that's the last time you come home with liquor on your breath. You wanna see all this disappear? Let me catch you with drugs in your purse. Let me find out you cheated on a test or ditched school. You wanna see magic? I can make this whole thing disappear. Just give me the excuse. Now go do what your mother says.

I mean, it's no "make him an offer he can't refuse," but it's the best I got.

Now, I'll admit, it's probably a lot easier if you're raising boys. Boys, you know what you're doing. They're pretty straightforward. You toss them a ball, you teach them how to watch for the pulling guards on the offensive line to know which way the halfback is going to run, you roughhouse with them a little bit, and when the time comes you give them money for condoms.

But if boys are like a Three Stooges movie, girls are a goddamn mystery novel. Not that I'm a big reader of mystery novels, but I'm sure if I was I'd figure them out about as easily as I can figure out daughters. Nevertheless, I do think I've learned a thing or two from raising two wonderful girls.

I'll tell you how I did it, and I'll also tell you how some friends of mine raised their kids. Because it's not as if I got all the answers, or any of them for that matter, but I have learned a lot from listening to guys who are a little smarter than me. Or at least a little less clueless.

I'll try to include some helpful hints on how to deal with

daughters, like what to do if they want to shave their heads (hint: No.), what to do if they want to date some high school dropout with a dagger tattoo on his face (hint: No way, what are you kidding me?), and what to do if she wants to pierce her nose (hint: Give me a fucking break).

Don't get me wrong. I'm no expert and I'm not trying to be. This is just the way I think, in my words, about my life with my kids. Did I do everything right? Not a chance in hell. Does anybody out there have a better idea? Most likely. My daughters are terrific, and they seem to be on a good path, knock wood. And if I had anything to do with that, then maybe I did something right.

Or maybe I just got lucky. And maybe that's the point: If we all share our stories about raising girls, maybe we'll figure out how to stretch our luck. Look, you're talking to a guy who worked in Vegas for twenty years. I've spent a lot of time in casinos, and if I learned anything there, I learned this:

You can't beat the house. But if you play your cards right, you can improve your odds a little bit.

This book is the story of how I played mine.

2

BABY MAKES THREE

You know how in the movies the wife tells the husband she's pregnant, and he takes a deep breath and gets a big smile on his face, and he hugs her and looks off camera high and to the left, like he's peering happily into the future?

Yeah, that wasn't me.

In 1991, I was working at the Riviera in Vegas. Making good money. Living the high life—I got off work at about two a.m., and that's a great moment in Vegas, it's like a second-wave party gets started as a lot of your friends get off work. Their pockets are stuffed with tips, and everybody wants to buy the first round. Me and my wife, Laura, had only been married a couple of years, but we'd been together a long time. Things were just great.

I was flush. I had the nice car, the big TV—big for those days, anyway. Nowadays people think you're chintzy unless you have a TV set the size of the Jumbotron at Yankee Stadium. We took lots of great vacations—first class, all the way.

It was on one of those vacations that it all happened. We

landed in Hawaii, and I made the same joke every dumb guy makes when he lands in Hawaii ("Hey babe, we're in Hawaii, how about a nice lei?"), and we headed to our hotel. That night, we had sea bass at this great little restaurant, and then every night after that my wife wanted to go to the same restaurant and have that same fish, it was so good.

Problem was, she started throwing up. I of course assumed it was the fish and was ready to go tear the chef a new one.

And then my wife said to me, Stevie, I don't think it's the fish.

I think it's a baby.

We got back to Vegas and she went to the doctor, and sure enough. It wasn't the fish.

I'm gonna be real honest. I was scared. Not for the reasons you're supposed to be scared, either: What if the baby is born with a terrible illness, what if I'm not a good father, what if I can't provide for my family?

My reaction:

Shit. The party's over.

Because a friend of mine had gotten married before me, and after the kid was born you never saw the guy again. I mean, I felt like, he was twenty-four, and then he had a kid, and he automatically became sixty-four. I've seen it happen too many times. I had just turned thirty-four, so in my world it was kinda late to get started on this parent thing. Most of my friends already had kids a long time ago; they had teenagers already, and I'd seen how their lives had changed. And everything in the culture supports that fear. Like the one on *Sex and the City* who has a baby and suddenly her part of the show is called "No Sex and No City."

So I was thinking, well, my life as I know it is over now.

We were in the middle of building this great big house at the time, a thirty-eight-hundred-square-foot house on an acre of land, and I'm sweating bullets. I'm worried, like any guy, about whether I got what it takes to support a family—not just financially, but everything else, too. Women don't seem to have those fears. I think that when girls are born, the doctor whispers, "Don't worry, one day, when you have kids, you'll be a great parent." When he slaps the babies to make them cry, they tell the dads that they did it to make sure the baby is breathing, but really, it's just to scare the shit out of you. So that's me and my wife: As she gets bigger and bigger, she gets calmer and calmer and I get more and more nervous.

So she's on her hands and knees with this big belly, picking out tiles for the new house, making cookies for the plumber, and acting like somehow having a baby is the most natural thing in the world.

Which, I guess, in the big scheme of things, it is. But you couldn't tell it from me.

Laura kept telling me that we were still gonna have our lives— we'd still go out, we'd still have fun. Only this way it would be more fun. I wanted to believe her. But you gotta imagine what it's like, having a baby in Vegas.

A lot of the guys I knew were married to showgirls—I'm not talking about strippers, I mean legit showgirls, dancers—and the guys all say the same thing: "If we have kids, we're gonna adopt. Are you kidding me? Look at my wife's body. That's some body, man. I'm not gonna ruin that body by letting her have a baby." And the wives say the same thing: "I have a baby, my career's over."

So, that's what passes in Vegas for a support system.

Those guys were about as wrong as wrong can be. My wife was in pretty good shape, anyways, but I didn't have any weird feelings when she started getting really large. For one thing, I don't care how many fights you've been in in your life, the first time you feel that baby kick inside your wife's belly, it's a knockout punch. You're on the floor, and you're not getting up for about another twenty years (if that. The feeling wears off, they tell me, about the time the baby graduates college. We've got that coming up, so I'll let you know). So you're so blown away by that, you can't possibly really be so small as to worry about whether your wife's butt looks big. Well, you can, I guess—guys can get pretty stupid about anything—but it sure didn't worry me. And besides, it's not like I'm one to talk about who's got a big butt around here, if you know what I mean.

Hand Out the Cigars with the Pink Ribbon

I wanna clear up one thing about guys and daughters right away. Everybody thinks every guy wants to have a little boy. But a scientific study conducted between me, my friend Richie, and this guy sitting next to us at the bar one time proves: It just ain't true.

It's something I figured out the first minute I held my first kid in my arms.

It was so strange, this kid I was holding for the first time. You imagine that you're going to have this little replica of you or your wife, like a tiny bobblehead is gonna come out with the name "Schirripa" on the base. This could have been a puppy, for all I could tell. She looked kind of like a cross between Yoda and Alfred Hitchcock.

I was so blown away, it actually took me a minute to register: She.

She looked like a cross between Yoda and Alfred Hitchcock.

Laura and I had decided not to learn the gender of the baby ahead of time—because, I guess, we figured there aren't enough surprises in store for us the day the baby is born. Let's make it even more mysterious.

We'd been up all night, and after the baby was born I stayed with my wife for a couple of hours, and then headed home to try to get some sleep, but I was so hopped up on the adrenaline and excitement of it all that I just stared at the ceiling and had my first minute to really think about it.

And I swear to God, I didn't feel disappointed that it wasn't a boy. Not one bit. In fact, I gotta say, I was kinda relieved.

As a kid growing up in a tough neighborhood, I knew how rough it can be on a boy. And not just the physical violence thing—everything. There's a lot of up and downs for guys that people don't talk about because guys are supposed to suck it up. But take sports, for example. Guys gotta be good at sports. I saw it from Little League on. Sports are a healthy thing, but they're a rough road, too.

You have a good game, the coach gives you a ride home; if you strike out three times, you're at the bus stop. For a ten-, twelve-year-old kid, that's heavy stuff.

I was a good athlete—I played basketball in college and held my own, but still, I knew how tough it could be on a guy.

So I was lying there, thinking, well, I'm glad it's a girl. Now it'll be easier.

Which shows you exactly how much I know.

Merry Christmas, Daddy

We brought the baby home just a few days before Christmas. Christmas is a surreal time in Vegas, and you never really get used to it, no matter how long you're there: Here are some strippers in tiny low-cut Santa suits with fishnet stockings, there's a Christmas tree with a great big gold dollar sign on top. And everything is gigantic—twenty-foot-tall Christmas trees, ten-foot-tall penguins in red scarves, wherever you look. The store window displays in Las Vegas are the size of entire shopping malls in other cities. So, you already feel like you're on some strange other planet. And then, every five seconds or so, it hits you again: You had a baby. You are a father.

I went out for a drink that night at a local bar with my friend Jimmy the Beak. He's a casino host, and his wife was seven months pregnant at the time, so he's looking at me for clues as to whether or not I'm terrified. Like playing poker: He's trying to find if I have a "tell." I keep saying I'm on top of the world, that I'm happy as a clam, but he's trying to figure out if I'm bluffing.

I'm trying to figure out the same thing.

But my fear that our lives were over turned out to be about as far off base as you can get. In fact, the very day Laura came home with little Bria, we had a huge Christmas party.

I shit you not. Maybe fifty people. We had planned the party a long way back—we always had a Christmas Eve party, every year—but when the baby came two days before the party, I asked Laura if we should just cancel it. And I think maybe she figured out that this was a good way to calm my fears about not having a life once the baby was born (although we wouldn't call it "calm my fears," exactly. We'd call it more like "getting Steve to shut the fuck up already").

We toasted everything—our new house, our new baby, our new life—and that night I went to bed feeling pretty good—a feeling that, for a dad, lasts exactly as long as it takes you to have this thought:

What if I fall asleep and roll over on the baby?

You know, they always used to pair a fat guy and a skinny guy together in comedy teams because they look so funny together. Laurel and Hardy. Abbott and Costello. Nikita Khrushchev and John Kennedy. But you put a big fat Italian and a tiny baby in the bed next to each other, and it's about as far from funny as you can get. Laura was breast-feeding, and sometimes in the night they'd both fall asleep afterward, and I'd be lying there with my eyes wide open like two big moon pies. I roll over on this kid, she doesn't stand a chance.

So I had plenty of time to be alone with my thoughts. And my main thought, in those early days was: Okay. We have a baby.

So what the fuck do I do now?

I kept thinking, isn't there a book of instructions they're supposed to give you when you leave the hospital? I mean really. You come home with a new Lincoln and you get more instruction on how to take care of it than when you come home with a new baby.

But we were pretty lucky. From the day we took her home, she woke up once a night, and that was it.

So here's the next rule for new dads: Get your hands dirty. And I mean, dirty. As in, change a goddamn diaper once in a while. Guys act like they don't know how to change a diaper. These are the same guys who can pull an engine out of a two-ton '92 Jeep Wrangler while drinking a beer and watching the ball game on a 12-inch TV they've had in the garage since the first Bush administration, and they can't change the diaper on a ten-pound baby? Please. And changing a diaper requires way, way less socket wrenches. Three or four, tops.

You know, I wasn't Father of the Year, but I was working nights and around the house all day, so what am I gonna do, sit on my ass and watch *The Price Is Right* while she's doing all the work?

Not that I don't love *The Price Is Right*. I mean, that's entertainment, and it's terrific that they're carrying on the time-honored work of the great Bob Barker, but really, who cares how much that dinette set goes for? I have a kitchen table already. Leave me alone.

I'll Have a Dewar's—the Baby Will Have a Borden's

I think Bria was about two weeks old when we brought her out to a restaurant. We had that little snap-out bassinet, so you could carry her around and put her down like a big turtle on its back (if the turtle was made out of bulletproof plastic and set me back a hundred bucks). Now, this pissed me off no end: The minute you sit down, you start getting the dirty looks.

Mind you, Bria was about the easiest baby you could imagine. As I said, almost from the beginning, she slept through the night. And when we'd take her out, she'd make less noise than the bartender when he's mixing a martini. But that didn't matter. Not only had I been thinking my days of leaving the house in the evening were over—but these people sitting at other tables in the restaurants were shooting us looks like, your life *should* be over.

So here's another good tip: Unless there's a sign out in front of the restaurant with a big picture of a baby on it and that red circle with the slash, then your money is as good as those shmucks who think they own the joint.

Establish this firmly in your mind from the get-go because it's only gonna get worse. Every parent has been in the situation where their toddler starts heaving a fit in the middle of the—well, you name it. The airport. The plane. The train. The restaurant. The Vatican. Our kids were great, but a kid's a kid, and they've had tantrums everyplace in New York. And parents freak out because they know they've got about three seconds from the time your kid starts screaming until the time you get The Look.

I don't understand it. What do those people think—oh, I was gonna let my kid scream until she passes out, but now that I know you're unhappy, I'll stop her right away? What, that I know exactly how to stop my kid from having a shit fit, but it hadn't occurred to me to do it until you gave me the evil eye?

Kids cry. Assholes act like assholes. So when your kid is crying in the restaurant, and some jerk shoots you The Look, just think to yourself, hey, this is okay. Everybody's just doing their job.

Now don't get me wrong—there are limits. I live in lower Manhattan, and I don't have any patience for these parents in the neighborhood who let their kids go running up and down the restaurant screaming their heads off. What, I'm paying $200 for a meal and I gotta watch the six-year-old Olympic games? I'm trying to enjoy my ziti and this kid is doing high dives off the corner booth? I don't think so. A baby starts to cry, okay, I get it, you can't lock the kid up in a closet until she's twenty-one (although that's not such a bad idea, which we'll get to later). It takes you a minute to find a pacifier? I get it. Your kids are playing stickball with a meatball and a loaf of Italian bread? It's time for an intervention.

Just the Two of Us

One thing I learned early on with Bria is that things are gonna happen in a certain order, and there's no stopping them, so you gotta pull your head out of the sand. The day is gonna come, sooner or later, when you're gonna be alone with the baby.

Now I know a lot of guys read that and say, "Okay, I'm prepared for that. I'll be alone with the baby. When she's like, twelve or so."

Which comes to one more new rule for the new dad:

Don't be such a pussy.

And when I say don't be such a pussy, I will add, because I'm an honest guy:

Don't be a pussy like me.

Laura hadn't worked since the baby was born, but when Bria was about six months old they were opening the new MGM

Grand, and they were going to hire the best-looking girls in town. It was going to be the toughest gig in the city to land. So of course, Laura lands it. Gets herself back into shape in about two seconds and lands a job as a cocktail waitress just like that.

It's not like we needed the money exactly, but I think it was more that she needed to know she could still get the gig. And guys need to know that women feel that way. It's not a reflection on you when your wife wants to go back to work. Not a reflection on whether you're a good enough earner, or on whether she wants to hang around and take care of the baby and wash your dirty under-wear all day, which of course who wouldn't want a gig like that? When your wife decides to go back to work, you gotta tell yourself, this one's not about you.

Until it is.

It becomes all about you when your wife decides to work days because you're working nights, which means one of you gets to be home with the baby all the time, which half the time, in my case, meant me.

Which in my case was terrifying.

Because I'm working like five o'clock until one or maybe two in the morning, and coming home, and she wakes up at eight a.m., and hands me the baby, and leaves.

Holy shit.

A lot of guys might love having their wives work—here we have this second income, which is making life really easy, and it's a decent income to boot; the MGM Grand people are no slouches—but not me. I'm begging her, every day, please, please, quit the job! I'm begging her mother, every day, to come over. I might be the only guy in the history of the United States to beg his mother-in-law to come over for coffee every day.

But nope. None of that. It was just me and the kid. All day, every day.

I went somewhere, I had the baby in the car seat. I'm hanging around the house, Bria is hanging with me.

Laura had left me a list of instructions. She was breast-feeding, which meant she used the pump thing. I never saw her do it—she went off into another room, and came back with a bottle filled with milk. She had a cow hidden back there, for all I knew.

But I had the bottles, and my list of instructions, and I'm pulling my hair out.

What the fuck do I do now?

Well boys, here's what I did.

I dealt with it.

I start going about my day, and pretty quickly I start going about my day with a baby on one arm. I learn to do a lot of things one-handed. After a couple of weeks, it's pretty amazing the things you can do with just one hand. Open a beer, check your e-mail, and whatever you're thinking right now, shut up you sick fuck. There's a baby in the room.

Fortunately, Laura had put me on a training schedule before she went back to work.

She would leave me alone with Bria for a couple of hours here or there. And we still had all these contractors around because the house wasn't completely done. And I've got the baby in one arm, and I'm yelling at contractors. And the guys who were handling the heating and the air-conditioning had their heads up their asses—they had to keep doing it over and over, and kept royally screwing up, and making one excuse after another. So one of them shows up one day, and I've got the baby in one arm, and she's crying her head off, and I start screaming at the contractor.

"What the hell is the matter with you?" I yell. "I've had enough of your bullshit to last me ten lifetimes. If you don't stop fucking around this minute, I'm gonna break your goddamn head wide open!"

And Bria, I swear to God, stops crying.

She's looking up at me, screaming my head off, like she's fascinated by what's going on. Now, I've never read a parenting book in my life (as will become pretty clear as we go along here), but I know a lot of people who read them like the Bible, and they assure me that none of these books advise, as a way to calm a crying baby, to scream your head off at an idiot contractor.

Then again, none of them were written by a Big Daddy.

I Gotta Be Me, You Gotta Be You

So like I said, the point is, if you're gonna be a dad, you still gotta be yourself. And me, I'm a nice guy. Until I'm not. My kids got used to me being who I am, and now it doesn't faze them. Just last Christmas we were all guests at a big show at a theater downtown, and as we're walking in this guy taps my daughter's bag with a long stick, and he's using the stick to go through the bag like he's giving it a colonoscopy, and I say, pretty politely (for me), "Excuse me, but what are you doing?" And he makes some snide remark, and like I said, I'm a nice guy until I'm not. And I start ripping this guy a new asshole, right in front of the Christmas tourist crowd, and my kids are just waiting patiently like I've handed the guy a twenty to get us to the head of the line.

And this is exactly how I am with my kids. I'm a nice guy until you give me a reason to get on your case. And then have no doubt that I will get on your case.

A lot of dads today have this idealized image of what a dad should be, based mostly on trying to be the opposite of whatever their own dad was.

My dad, not to put too fine a point on it, was a screw-up.

I come from a dysfunctional house. Five kids who grew up on

welfare. Poor as shit. My mother held us together, but my father tore us apart.

My father was a small-time wise guy. He got arrested a couple of times and did a couple of stints for bookmaking and other stuff. But he wasn't very good at it. He got out after a while, but he wasn't any good at anything else either. He had every job in the world, bartending at Shea Stadium, working at the horse track—and was fired for stealing, every time. Sometimes he lived with us, and sometimes he just disappeared for months at a stretch.

He didn't hit us—too often, anyway—but he screamed and yelled and cursed all the time. My mother did her best, and she was a loving mom, but I never got over the fact that she took all the bullshit my father doled out. And the humiliation of being the kid on welfare really stung. I remember always having to go up to the store with a note—"Please give my son food and I'll pay you later"—and standing there while the grocer read the note, and waiting to find out if he was going to say yes or no. Or going to the store with food stamps—I've never used a coupon in a grocery store, to this day, because they bring back the memory of those food stamps.

I mean, when my father was around, he'd ask me for a dime to buy the paper. Can you imagine? Man's your father, and literally, literally, doesn't have a dime to his name.

After school sometimes I had to wait in line at a storefront in the neighborhood for a hunk of government cheese and some canned goods, and worry that some kids from my class at school were gonna walk by and see me in that line. It makes my cheeks burn just remembering it.

Like all kids, I was out of the house a lot of the day—after school, and on the weekends. You just went out by yourself and hung around. And given some of the characters in my neighborhood, I gotta say, how I wound up not falling into the wrong way of life, I have no clue. For whatever reason, one guy goes right and one guy goes left. And I knew a lot of guys who went down the wrong path.

I played ball, and maybe that helped me keep it together. But look: I got a friend of mine, grew up right across the street from me, been in jail the last twenty-five years. Some of the kids on the block have been murdered, and some of the kids on the block committed murder themselves. One buddy of mine—nice guy, good stickball player, gave you a quarter for a soda once in a while. Open the paper, and see that his father killed six people.

Bensonhurst was pretty mobbed up in those days, and it didn't take much to find yourself a little dirty business to get involved in; I was broke, and it was tempting, so how I didn't go there, who the hell knows.

But I did know this.

When I had kids, it was going to be different.

I mean, some things are pretty obvious lessons: Don't scream stupid shit at your wife in front of the kids. Don't kill six people. If possible, try not to be a bum who disappears for months at a stretch and can't provide for his family worth a shit.

But the most important lesson was just—Be There.

Of all the rules we're talking about, that's the one that sticks with me the most, when I think about my own childhood.

I may do things right and I may do things wrong.

But I am going to Be There.

Big, and loud, and present.

And my kids know they can take that to the bank.

For a lot of guys my age, I know, the image they have of their dad is not like mine was. And God bless them for that. But the dads of our parents' generation were still pretty distant and uninvolved. And when they were involved, they didn't allow for much argument. When I talk to guys my age, they tell me that their dads said, "Do it because I said so," and so they vowed they'd never say that to their own kids.

If anything defines dads today, it's that need to be different from their own dads, the need not to be the guy who says, "Do it because I said so."

Well, you know what? I say, "Do it because I said so" is the best tool in a dad's toolbox. Next to the socket wrenches for changing the diapers, I mean.

Years ago, Bria, who had her ears pierced, wanted to get a second hole in her ear. We were out to dinner with my mother, and Bria mentioned it. And my mother said, "Steven, why don't you let her get it?"

And what I said was, "Because I don't want her to."

And it goes back and forth. "But why don't you want her to?" And I said, "Because I don't want her to, that's why I don't want her to. I don't have to have a reason."

Now, it was strange for me to be having this argument with my mother. For me to be telling her, "It's because I said so." It's weird to change roles with your mother like that. But I was glad for the argument to come up, because it's important for Bria to know that sometimes she can't do things. And she can't do them because I said so.

I don't know why parents have become so afraid of telling their kids, "Because I said so." It really is the most underrated sentence in a dad's vocabulary.

And for those of you who wanna tell me that "because I said so" is not, in fact, a sentence, shut the fuck up.

This is what it means to be a Big Daddy. And it's what's missing from a lot of the relationships between dads and their kids today. And if there's one reason for me writing this book, other than it's just the right size to put under the wobbly table you have in the garage, it's to say: It's not only okay to be the Big Daddy, it's fucking necessary. Because things have gotten out of hand.

Kids from the moment they can shake their head from side to side will challenge you. Not because they are lunatics (which they are) or because they are selfish (which they are, times ten), but because they want to know where you draw the line, so they know not to walk past it. You know those electric dog collars that give the dog a shock every time it reaches the end of the yard, so it learns not to go in the street and get hit by the UPS truck?

You should put one of those collars on your kid.

Not literally (although it would save on the babysitting bills later). But you gotta be like that dog collar. When the dog reaches the end of the yard, it gets a shock. The dog doesn't say to the collar, "Well, why can't I go farther than the end of the yard?" and the collar doesn't say, "Well, dear, because you will be hit by the UPS truck," and the dog doesn't say, "But there's no UPS truck coming," and the collar doesn't say, "Well, but there could be a UPS truck coming. Or maybe FedEx," and the dog doesn't say, "Well, what if I only go in the street when there are no trucks coming?" and the collar doesn't say, "Well, there could be some other vehicle coming, like a blue station wagon," and the dog doesn't say, "Well, can I go past the yard just this once?" and the collar doesn't say, "Well, just this once, but only as far as the sidewalk," and on and on.

The collar doesn't bargain.

The dad shouldn't bargain either.

How do you know this is true?

Because I said so.

As Frightening as It Gets

A buddy of mine, Lon Bronson, had one of the earliest Big Daddy moments I know. Lon and I go way back—he and I worked on a show together back in February 1985. Great guy. Really good-looking wife—she was Lance Burton's levitation girl in his magic shows for years. We all were living large back in those days, and Lon and his wife weren't ready to have kids—but when they did finally get around to it, it really changed their lives. Now, understand that when you're in a band in Las Vegas, and your wife's in a big show, the parties are never-ending. And they're really wild. There's not a lot that can top that.

Until your daughters are born.

"They're both just really, really cool little girls," he said when we talked a little while ago. "I'd have to say the biggest deal with me is, we're really good friends, but it's not one of those friendships where they take advantage of me and don't respect me. I like to think they think I'm a cool dad, but we really get along and I look forward to spending time with them. 'What am I gonna do? Oh, it's the weekend! I get to hang out with the girls!' It's evolved from that place where my wife and I were like, 'Where's the next party, what are we doing, we're going to some concert, we're gonna hang out,' to 'Oh boy, what are we gonna do with the girls this weekend?' Honestly, I've had so much more fun the last fourteen years, hanging out with my girls, than I did in the first ten years of big-party Vegas. There's not even a comparison. And I'm talking, there's a lot of crazy shit that went down in those years. Was that fun? Yeah. But it doesn't even compare."

Amen to that, brother. I feel the same way, in spades.

Anyway, both of Lon's daughters had some medical scares when they were born—they both turned out perfectly fine, thank God—but it's the moment that you really have to deal with who you are as a dad.

With his first daughter, Alana, the doctors came to him and said they saw a little shadow on the X-ray that could be nothing.

Or it could be a hole in her heart valve.

How do you deal with that information? "You're as wiped out as you get," Lon told me. "You're devastated. There's nothing that can prepare you for this. And there's nothing that compares with this."

The problem is, as a dad, you just want to fix things. I don't care what it is—what the problem is—you know you wanna get in there and make it right. And when you can't—when you feel helpless—there's no way to deal with that. It just short-circuits your brain.

Like I said, God bless, with Alana, it turned out to be nothing. But with the second daughter, Taylor, they go through it again. This time it's something called the bilirubin level, which is something in the blood that if it is high can turn your baby a deep yellow color and they get really sleepy and sick. So the levels are high, and right away they're putting the kid in the preemie ward, even though she's like nine pounds, and they're poking her with the needle every few hours to check her blood.

So Lon is looking down at his daughter, his beautiful wonderful incredible new daughter, on the first day of her life, and she's miserable. Screaming to high heaven every time they poke her in the heel with that needle.

The third time he sees them coming, he says, you know what? Enough is enough.

He steps in front of the doctor, the nurse, and the needle.

"No more blood," he says. "You're done for today."

They look at him like he's nuts. And he figures, maybe he is. But this is the decision he made. "Look, I know you're trying to help my daughter, and I appreciate that. But she's one day old, and you're torturing her. Give her a break. You got enough blood for now."

The nurse doesn't even argue. She clearly knows she's not gonna win. All of a sudden, they come up with a new plan, and wrap the kid in some kind of silver solar blanket like she's on a pizza delivery truck, and stick her in the incubator with some heat lamps, and a couple of days later, the kid is fine.

Did he do the right thing? Hell if I know. Probably not. I mean, the kid is a day old and you're challenging the doctors? That takes balls the size of coconuts. But did he do the Big Daddy thing? Absolutely. He decided somebody was hurting his daughter, and when you're a Big Daddy, nobody hurts your daughter. Nobody. I don't care how smart they are or how good their intentions are. That's the thing—when you're the Big Daddy, you do what your gut tells you to do, right or wrong, and when it comes to protecting your kids, you are the fucking immovable object.

I get where he's coming from. Because I feel exactly the same way. You wanna hurt my kid, you gotta go around me.

And in my case, that's a long way to go.

You know, when my kids went to school in Vegas, they went to this private school, and one of the administrators was like a bad used-car salesman. It was torture to listen to this guy—and he talked every chance he got. Very full of himself. My nephew also went to the school, and I can't remember what my nephew did, but this administrator shows him a paddle and says, "The next time you do that, I'm gonna paddle you."

This story gets back to me pretty quick, and I immediately flash back—I remember when I was in school, the teacher slapped me. A bunch of times. One time I remember, I threw an eraser at my friend, and he ducked, and it hit this girl smack in the face. With the chalk on her face, she looked like a raccoon. So the teacher takes me outside and slaps me, very deliberately.

So you think I'm gonna let a teacher lay a finger on my kids? They're terrified, my two little girls, by this goddamn idiot. I don't even know if he really would ever paddle a kid or not, but that's not the point. To even use the threat of physical violence against my children—that's absolutely unacceptable.

And that's absolutely the moment when Big Daddy needs to step in.

I sat my kids down, and my nephew too, and I told them, "If

this guy lays one finger on you, I'm gonna give you my word, if he paddles you, I'm gonna come to school, I'm gonna pull his pants down, and I'm gonna paddle him in front of all of you."

You're not gonna paddle my kids, you're not gonna paddle anyone I know. That's not gonna happen. Am I overprotective of my kids? Damn right I am. And I'm just getting warmed up.

Where It Starts

For me, I think the whole business of being overprotective started the moment my first daughter was born. I remember I was planning to be in the delivery room when the baby came, and all my friends are saying, what are you, nuts? Especially Italian guys. I'm actually half Italian and half Jewish, so I get it both ways. Crazy and full of guilt, both at the same time. Two for one. But a lot of my Italian friends, they're all saying to me, if I saw my wife having a baby, I could never touch her again. I see a head coming out of that, I'm never going back in there. The ones who did it were disgusted, and the ones who didn't were sure they would have been.

But you know what? Not only wasn't it disgusting, or gross, or frightening—well, let's not go too far. It was pretty frightening. But my point is, it was great, too. Being there. I wouldn't have missed it for anything, and if I had it to do ten more times, I'd be there ten more times.

(Not that we're planning to do this ten times. I may be Catholic but I'm not *that* Catholic. God bless those people with ten kids; I grew up with a lot of big Italian families in the neighborhood, and there's a lot of love in those houses. But there's also a lot of years of shitty diapers. We went through it twice and figured that was plenty.)

We almost didn't make it to the hospital, by the way. The day my wife went into labor we had this neighbor over the house, telling us some cockamamie story about how she was suing her neighbor for hanging their laundry over their property line, and we told her we had to go—like, *now*—and she wouldn't shut up. (That's your next big show-business tip. When someone tells you her water broke, say, "Thank you, ladies and gentlemen, you've been a lovely audience. Good night!" and get the hell out of there.) Besides, who the hell hangs their laundry out to dry anymore? What, you can't spring for an electric dryer? Although I should say, when I was growing up, everybody had a clothesline outside their window. Kids spent their days with ladies' underwear flying over their heads like the Italian flag. There were some ladies in the neighborhood whose bras and panties had their own national anthem.

We get to the hospital and we've already beeped Laura's folks—this was a little before every human walking the earth had their own portable phone booth in their pocket, hard as it is for my kids to even imagine; but everyone had a beeper, like we'd suddenly turned into a nation of crack dealers. We really don't give crack dealers the credit they deserve, by the way: I don't think the cell phone industry would have ever taken off without them. They were true pioneers.

So Laura's mom is there when we get there. We didn't videotape the birth, although we did for our second daughter. By your second kid, you're so relaxed, you invite everybody—Laura's parents were there, a friend of ours, the baby's godmother, and she was filming the whole thing, and so probably she had a sound man and gaffer and key grip with her—it was a goddamn party already. You couldn't tell if Laura was giving birth to a baby or a reality TV show.

But with our first kid, Bria, it was just me and Laura and her mom in the room, and for all the Lamaze classes and Birthing Together lectures that we went to—and I went to all that shit—you get in the room and you find out what a dad's real job is. There are two, actually.

One is, you hold this little pan next to your wife's head, so if she wants to throw up during the process we don't have to disturb any of the nurses, who have much more important things to do.

And two, you're in charge of imagining every possible thing that can go wrong.

What if something goes wrong? What am I supposed to do? It's like that dream everybody has that you're back in school and there's a big test and you didn't study, or you're about to go out on-stage but you forgot to read the lines. Only a thousand times more serious. And everyone's looking at you. And you're standing there with your thumb up your ass.

The doctor kept reassuring us that everything was going to be okay. Of course, in our case, this guy happens to be the same doctor who is later indicted for defrauding people with incurable diseases by telling them he was going to give them a miracle cure by injecting them with tissue from placentas. So you never know. In Vegas, everybody's got a story.

So when the baby comes out, and you hear that cry, there's no greater sound in the world. Laura's dad told me to count the fingers and toes—it's one of those nutty things parents do to reassure themselves. Of all the things that could be wrong in your life, having six toes doesn't sound like it's high on the list, but it's the easiest thing to check for right then and there (if dads could say, "Check to see if they're going to crash the car when they're eighteen, so I know whether to get a lower deductible," they would do that, but they can't, so they go for the fingers and toes thing).

But that's when it started, for me. I started worrying from that moment. I was in charge of figuring out everything that could go wrong, and I was responsible—in my own head—for making sure it didn't.

Twenty years later, I'm still doing the same thing: imagining every possible thing that could go wrong for my two beautiful girls and, come what may, doing whatever I can to make sure it doesn't happen.

Do I drive them nuts?

Absolutely.

Is there a chance in hell I'm gonna stop?

Absolutely not.

Once you're a Big Daddy, you're a Big Daddy for life.

3

DADDY'S LITTLE GIRLS

When it comes to little girls, let's face it. Dads are toast.

No matter how you try, you can't help it. They look up at you with those big eyes, and you just melt, like a Good Humor ice cream somebody dropped on the sidewalk in the middle of July.

So part of being a Big Daddy is learning to resist. Because that's a big part of the problem. These dads who give their kids everything? All they're really teaching their kids is the idea that the world is going to meet their every need. I got this friend, I'm at his house, and the little girl is lying on the couch watching TV and announces to the world, "I need cereal." And the dad, without a moment of hesitation, gets up and goes to the cupboard and gets down the Froot Loops.

First of all, I'm no health freak, as should be easy to figure out just by looking at the picture on the cover of this book, but really? Froot Loops? What, you're hoping that if you feed the kid pure sugar, the rush will be enough to get her up off that couch so you can turn off the TV for five minutes?

Second of all, this kid has been watching TV since the sun came up. The screen is bigger than she is. She's living in that world with Dora the Goddamn Explorer and that stupid talking map, which, thank God, didn't come along until my kids were too old for it, because I would have thrown a shoe through the damn TV. Go get some fresh air, for Chrissakes! That's the good thing about the DVR. You can pause Dora and come back later. About five years later would be a good time, if you ask me.

But to get back to the point: The kid announces, "I need cereal." The dad, like someone pushed a button in his back, goes to get the cereal. No thought that maybe the kid should ask him, or say please, or, God forbid and the house should fall down around his ears, she should learn to get it for herself. So a six-year-old might spill the milk once in a while. Or might get distracted on the way to the Froot Loops and wind up with a cookie instead, which probably has more nutrition than the Froot Loops anyway. (Fuck, I think that instead of eating the Froot Loops, the kid would be better off eating the box they came in.)

It's that big-eyes thing. Little girls have this ability to hypnotize their dads—they don't even have to swing the watch in front of your face. They just give you that look, and you melt.

Unless you don't.

Unless you know, like every Big Daddy knows, the secret to unlocking the mystery of the little girl.

Which I learned from my friend Anson Williams.

Anson became famous for playing the character Potsie on *Happy Days*, one of the biggest TV shows of all time. What everybody doesn't know is that, in addition to becoming a great director—among other things, Anson directed some episodes of *Secret Life of the American Teenager*, and he's one of the best directors I've ever worked for—he also became the father of five, count 'em, five daughters.

"Five daughters," he told me, "so I know two things. One, God is getting even with me for everything I did in the seventies. And two, God is a woman."

Five daughters. So when it comes to learning the ways of the American girl, Anson's your man.

First lesson from Anson is learning the difference between boys and girls. "It's the difference between living with Pee Wee Herman and Einstein," he said. "Boys are simple. Boys are easy. Girls are complex. They're really smart. But they're really, really cunning, too."

And they know exactly how to get what they want. Boys kind of bob along the day, like a cork you dropped in the fish tank, just floating and bouncing off of things. Girls are always plotting. You gotta know that. Because it's true.

Case in point: Anson told me that he and his wife had a little spat one day. Nothing big, just the kind of thing that a husband and wife who live in a crazy house with five young kids get to arguing about. He retreated to his office.

His littlest daughter, who is five, shares a room with one of her older sisters; the older one doesn't hear the argument, but the little one does.

She comes into Anson's office and climbs up in his lap. Oh, how cute, Anson thinks. She's trying to make me feel better.

"Daddy?" she says, giving him the big eyes. Size of silver dollars by now. Should have been his first clue.

"Yes, dear?" he says.

"Daddy," she says, "if you and Mommy get a divorce, can I make your office into my bedroom?"

Plotting. Planning. And it never stops. The further along they go, Anson says, the more cunning they get. And the more complicated.

Nothing's ever simple with a girl.

"Here's how it goes," Anson says. "Dad to Boy:
'Let's go play ball.'
'Uh, okay.'
'Want a burger?'
'Uh, okay.'
'Go to bed.'
'Uh, okay.'
Dad to Girl:
'Let's go play ball.'
'What color is the ball? How long are we going to play for? Can we go to the mall after we play? How long do we have to play ball before we go to the mall? Can I get some shoes?'"

Anson found some candy hidden in one of the girls' rooms the other day. With a boy, it would have been, "Yeah, sorry, Dad." With his girls, it was an hour-long inquisition. "And I never did figure it out," he said. "They had me so spun around, I forgot what we were arguing about."

So yeah, you gotta be on your toes around girls—especially when they get to be teenagers, which Anson has a lot to say about, and I'll get to that later—but there's one other thing he told me about being the dad of young girls that's really, really important.

And it's what he says he learned because he's an older dad.

Anson was forty when his first daughter was born and fifty-eight for his youngest. He says that when you're an older dad, you may not have the energy to keep up with your kids—it's a helluva lot more exhausting—but what you give up in endurance, you make up for in patience. And perspective.

"By the time we had kids, I was so ready, so focused," he said. "When you're younger, all this other stuff seems so important. Getting this job, reaching that goal, being the top in the market-place. All that stuff. And yet what you're sacrificing is the time with your family. It's someone's foundation, someone's desperate need to connect with their parent.

"By the time we had kids, my priorities were so different. It's so much clearer what's important. What I do now, it's not for me, it's for them. They're not interfering with my success—they're not interfering with anything, other than making me totally exhausted. But it's worth it. Because I have more wonderment at this age. Having all this youth around me."

That's a Big Daddy talking—because what Anson gets, and what any guy ought to get, is that once you have kids, it's not about you anymore. It's about them. And that's not a bad thing.

So every night, whatever the hell else is going on, and no matter how much chaos is going on—and in a house with five girls, there's plenty—Anson and his wife, Jackie, make sure everybody sits around the table at dinner together. Together. Everything else stops. No one takes a phone call. No one checks an e-mail. No one is texting. They're there. They go around the table, and each person tells "what was my best of the day." And everybody listens.

And when the little one's turn comes, she tells her best of the day to her dad. And she gives him the big eyes.

And of course, he melts, like that Good Humor bar.

And sometimes that's not a bad thing, either.

To the Princess Belongs the Spoils

I'll tell you who spoils his kids. My buddy Joe Piscopo. I think he's a great dad. But boy, do his kids have him wrapped around their little fingers. Especially his thirteen-year-old daughter.

"I'm not a good disciplinarian, " Joe admitted. "Especially with the girls. You cuddle them, you treat them like princesses."

Case in point: Just a couple of weeks ago. "My daughter, my thirteen-year-old, she goes, I want to meet Justin Bieber," Joe told me. "So I make the call. This kid works more than anybody. He's about to play before twenty thousand people at the Izod Center.

I orchestrate a meet and greet. So, we go, he's there. He just did a Barbara Walters interview, he's about to play before twenty thousand live, and he takes the time to talk with my daughter and take a picture. We take one, two, three pictures—if it was me, I would have said, 'All right already.'"

Bieber leaves to go onstage, and Joe looks to his daughter for approval. To his amazement, she seems disappointed.

"Oh," she says. "I thought we were going to hang out with him."

You know the speech we always got from our parents—about how you should be grateful for what you have? Yeah, Joe doesn't exactly give that speech.

"Now, I should say, 'Honey, do you know how lucky you are to get close to this guy? One of the biggest teen idols in the world?' But no. Now it's on my agenda, I'm working on there being an opportunity where my daughter can, in fact, hang out with Justin Bieber. This is how I spoil my kids."

Big Daddy Riddle: Guess Who's in Charge Here

Like I said, I think Joe is a great dad, and I don't want it to sound like I'm busting his balls about spoiling his kids. He's actually a lot more in charge than he says he is. I know from watching him. But I do wanna say that all of this comes back to making it really clear who is running the show. Letting the kids know who is in charge is a big Big Daddy rule for me, and it's one you can't start early enough. I remember with Ciara, maybe she was about five or six, she walked into the room one night, and I was watching TV with my business manager, Roger. Roger's more than my business manager, really—he's a friend who handles everything for me, all the finances, all the big decisions, and he's really like an extension of the family. Anyway, we're hanging out, and Ciara walks in the room and just changes the channel.

I tell her, You can't do that. Daddy's watching TV.

But I want to watch TV, she says. It isn't fair.

I don't raise my voice, but I say to her, listen. This is all my stuff. You see everything here? This is all my stuff. Everything you see. It's mine. The furniture, the house, the TV, it's all mine. Because I pay all the bills.

She doesn't miss a beat. "You don't pay all the bills," she said. "Roger pays all the bills."

So okay. So maybe she didn't get the lesson that day. But the point is, I gave it my best shot. She'll learn soon enough, I figured. I'll make sure of that.

How to Get Your Kid to Act Like Less of an Idiot

I'll tell you something else that I taught my kids when they were little. It seems like a stupid little thing, but I was a fanatic about it, and now that they're older, I'm glad that I was.

I taught them to look adults in the eye when they talked to them.

I don't know why that's so hard for parents. Yeah, you have a three-year-old, he's talking to you and rolling on the floor and chewing on the dog's ear, I get that. But at some point you gotta stop that behavior. Drives me nuts.

Take Bria, though. By the time she was five years old, we'd go to a restaurant and she could look the waiter in the eye and place her order. Now, fifteen years later, I can see it in the way she deals with people. She's assured, she's direct. Is she the world's best student? No. She's pretty good, and getting better all the time. But I know a lot of kids who are book smart who can't carry on a conversation with an adult for two seconds. Where the hell are those kids' parents, and what the hell are these kids gonna do when they get their first job? You see it all the time. You go to a business and right up front you have kids who don't know enough to put their damn phone call on hold when they're talking to you. Kids who can't look you in the eye while they're performing the one function they have on earth, which is to say, "Someone will be right out."

It goes back to the parents. Like I said, I hear the way parents let their kids talk to them, and it's crazy. That whiny, self-involved voice. The one that says, the world is annoying to me, but if you buy me this thing, maybe I'll be able to contain my annoyance for a few minutes.

Right. That'll last a long time around Big Daddy. Two seconds sounds about right.

And that reminds me. There's one other thing kids do? When they're talking? To you? Which is, to talk in all questions? Like this? All day?

Yeah, that. As long as we're solving all the problems of the world, let's put that one on the list. It's another one that makes my teeth ache.

They say it's an insecurity thing. That kids are doing that because they're looking for reassurance when they're talking.

I think that's bullshit. I think it's a habit that kids get into—like snapping their gum or tapping their foot or biting their nails—and the only way to stop it is to stop it.

I heard this one dad in a restaurant: He was working on his kid. Relentless.

"Dad?"

"Are you asking me if I'm your dad?"

"No. Dad. I was in school yesterday?"

"Are you asking me if you were in school yesterday?"

"No. I know I was in school. I'm saying, I was in school yester-day. And Nicky comes up to me?"

"You want to know if Nicky came up to you? I can call Nicky if you like."

"No. Dad! So Nicky came up to me?"

"I have Nicky's mom's number if you really need to know."

I don't know if this dad ever cured his kid of question-itis, but I like to think that he did. Either way—big hand for the Big Daddy. It's not about winning the point—it's about making the effort.

More Frightening Shit

The hard part of having little girls, for me, is trying not to freak out about how dangerous the world is around them. You watch them like a hawk, every second. And it's exhausting.

When I was growing up, you got up in the morning, you made yourself a bowl of cereal, you watched a little TV, you got dressed, and you got the hell out of the house. Your mom asked you where you were going, and you said, "Out," and she told you what time to come back, and you were out the door. Kids were pretty much on their own.

It's a way different world now.

Maybe it was always dangerous and we didn't know it, or maybe the world has actually gotten a lot more dangerous, but ei-ther way, the things our parents did—like actually letting us be out of their sight for more than two minutes—would get you hauled before Child Protective Services today.

There are so many things you have to talk to your kids about that our parents didn't. Like why you have to wear protective headgear for any activity faster than walking. I mean, come on. Can you imagine when we were kids, if you went out roller skating, and your mother made you put on a helmet, how long it would take before you got beat up? I'd say the over-under on that is about no seconds.

And food. Kids grow up today thinking that a can of Coke is more dangerous than napalm, that eating white bread is worse for you than eating the wrapper it comes in, and that Twinkies will make you insane. Well, maybe the Twinkies part is true, but for the rest of it, I mean really. It's too much.

But of all the things you have to deal with that our parents never talked to us about, the toughest is a term we never even heard of when we grew up.

Child abduction.

Our parents told us not to talk to strangers, which didn't make any sense, because what were you going to do, go into a candy store to get a soda, and the guy behind the counter asks you what you want, and you go, "Sorry, my mother told me not to talk to strangers"? But the idea of why you had to not talk to strangers—that there were people out there who kidnap kids for evil purposes—didn't actually come up.

These days, every parent has to learn how to talk to their kids about "stranger danger." The guy who's helping me write this book used to produce the show *America's Most Wanted*, and he drove his kids nuts. Every time a kid got snatched anywhere in the country, his stepdaughter had to hear about it. What the kidnapped kid did right, what she did wrong, what you should do in that situation. She was the only fourth grader in her school who knew what to do if you get locked in the trunk of a car. (For the record, you pull out the wires from one of the brake lights, so you can hope that the guy gets pulled over by a cop for having a taillight out; if you can, smash out one of the taillights and wiggle your fingers at the car behind you. See, who knew this when we were growing up? And I was in a pretty tough neighborhood, where guys got thrown in the trunks of cars all the time. But usually they were in no condition to wiggle their fingers, or any other part of their body, if you get my drift. But that's a different story.)

Anyway, the worst case I ever heard of was my friend Billy, who actually showed his kid this *Stranger Danger* video they have out. The basic instruction for the kid is, if some guy grabs you in a public place and tries to force you out the door, you fall on the floor and scream, as loud as you can, "THIS IS NOT MY DADDY!" They even practiced it at home, like the video said they should, so the kids would get the idea that in this instance it's acceptable to scream at the top of your lungs.

They had a good laugh and a hug when it was all over, and my buddy Billy went to sleep thinking, what a good dad am I.

Proof of just how wrong dads can be sometimes.

About a month later they stopped at one of the rest stops on the New Jersey Turnpike, because you can never get your kids enough greasy horrible food. He picked up some big lollypops on the way out, and as he handed them to the girls, the younger one, who was about four, decided that this would be a great moment to try out what she had learned.

"THIS IS NOT MY DADDY!" she screamed. Billy tried to quiet her down, which only made her scream more. She kept shouting, "THIS IS NOT MY DADDY!" and was giddy with glee.

Unfortunately, "glee" was not what it seemed like to the group of New Jersey state troopers and park rangers sitting at the next table.

Suddenly, all attention is focused on the guy coming up to the two young girls, holding two giant lollypops.

As the state troopers start walking in their direction, Billy panics. He decides to try to cut this off as quickly as possible, and shouts out the first thing that comes into his mind, which is, unfortunately:

"Of course I'm your daddy! Why else would I be buying you candy? Now let's get back into the van and go!"

It's not often that dads get to learn how strong state troopers are.

So my point is: Yes, you have to teach your kids to be careful out there. You just gotta be careful about how you teach them.

Two Doors, No Good Choices

If you're the father of little girls, sooner or later you're going to take them out into the world, and sooner or later they're going to have to do what little girls have to do, and sooner or later you're gonna confront the question every father confronts:

How the hell do I take them to the bathroom?

You stand between the two doors, one with that picture of a woman in a triangular skirt, the other with the drawing of a guy who looks like he got flattened by a steamroller, and you think, okay, there's a men's room and a women's room, but no guy-with-little-girls' room.

Think fast.

It takes about two seconds to realize you can't go into the ladies'. And it takes about two nanoseconds to realize you don't want to take them into the men's.

My buddy Tony's first encounter with taking his daughter to the men's room may not have scarred the girl for life, but it sure scarred Tony: "Look!" his four-year-old yelled. "They all have those things that hang off on boys!"

You decide up front that you just don't care if you're making the men uncomfortable; they can handle it (while they're handling whatever they're handling). And you decide you could make a mint if you put a patent on blinders for little girls.

But that's not the worst of it.

Let's face it. Guys are gross. We can live with that. But the public men's room at, say, a train station, is about the most disgusting place on the face of the earth.

My advice: Get over it. Your kids will live.

A lot of guys freak out at this. My buddy Billy, the same guy with the state troopers I told you about, is a germ freak. The first time he took his girls to the men's room alone was at *Disney on Ice* at Madison Square Garden. The smell reminded him of a used diaper storage facility in the Sudan. While he was busy with his five-year-old, covering the toilet for her with enough paper to print the Sunday *New York Times*, his three-year-old was busy washing her hands in the conveniently positioned funny-looking sink (which the rest of us call a "urinal"). The cool thing for her was not only was there already warm water in there, but she was able to retrieve the big white piece of candy that someone had left at the bottom.

So he takes the girls into a stall with him, and locks the door, and has them stand behind him (and if you've ever tried to take a leak with two little kids in the stall with you, you know that can take a minute). Unfortunately, the older girl was already a good reader. So:

" 'Here I sit, brokenhearted . . .'"

"What?" asked Tony.

" 'Paid my dime and only farted'? What does that mean?"

"Where did that come from?"

"That's what it says on the wall."

"Well, stop reading that."

"Dad, what does N-A-N-T-U-C-K-E-T mean?"

At that moment, the sounds of a large walrus trying to mate or battle with a blue whale erupted from the adjacent stall. At least that's what it sounded like. It was followed by a series of rapid-fire machine-gun-like blasts. For a second there was silence, then the girls erupted with hysterical laughter. Laughter that just wouldn't stop. Laughter that would not allow them to stand upright any longer. They rolled on the disgusting floor, laughing hysterically.

Bill was mortified, and sure that the guy in the next booth would come out and deck him. But the point is:

The girls had the right idea.

Being a dad means getting into ridiculous situations you never expected to get into. You take them too seriously, you'll drive yourself crazy. It's not gonna scar your daughter for life to walk into a room full of men taking a leak—unless you make a big deal of it. Kids are resilient. Dads gotta be, too.

Great Moments in Big Daddy History

My buddy Lon had to confront another Big Daddy situation when his daughter was about five. We all go through this. But we don't all go through it as smart as Lon did.

They'd started the older daughter, Alana, on the violin when she was five. Lon's a big-time musician, so he knows all the arguments about whether it's better to start a kid early on music, or whether it's bad to start them too early. In this case, he figured, it was probably too early, because from the beginning she didn't want to practice. She was complaining a lot—the kid and the violin weren't a match made in heaven. But they made it to her first recital. While she was sitting there, waiting to go up on stage and play "Hot Cross Buns," she was restless. Couldn't sit still. Finally— Lon's not sure how she did it, but he looks down, and the bridge of the violin is broken, so the strings are sitting right against the frets.

"Daddy," she says, with the big pouty eyes, "my violin broke." (This is total kid language, by the way. Whenever something happens, it's not, "I broke it." It's just, "It broke." I don't know where kids get religion so fast, but something breaks, and suddenly it's an act of God.) "I can't play it, Daddy. I can't."

"This is a moment of parenting decision," Lon says to me later, "because a lot of parents, I'm sure, would have said, 'Oh, you broke the violin, it's game over.' But then I'm thinking, 'You know what, I think there's resistance here. I think she didn't want to do the recital at all. I think this could be a moment where she needs to face her fear. And I know this is a tough decision and I know a lot of people are going to look at this decision as being heartless.' But I said, 'You go up there and you play "Hot Cross Buns" as best you can.'"

And she started to cry.

This is the toughest moment for a Big Daddy. You just want to make it better. You just want the tears to go away. And mostly, you don't want all the other parents thinking, "What's wrong with this asshole? What's he doing to his kid?"

But you also don't want your kids to learn that you get to just back out of anything you feel like. And is five years old too early to start to learn that? I don't think so.

Lon doesn't give in. Alana's turn comes; she's stopped crying. She climbs up on the stage and scratches her way through "Hot Cross Buns." Not the best she ever did it; not the worst of any kid there that day, by any stretch. Certainly set the record for Best Version of Hot Cross Buns Ever Played on Broken Violin.

And most important, she learned something.

She learned that you don't back down. You don't walk away.

Fast-forward about seven years. Now Alana's going into junior high school, and she has to make a decision on whether to get into the band. "No way," she says. "Band is for dorks."

This drives his dad crazy for two reasons. One, he immediately thinks she's been brainwashed by the Disney Channel. My kids don't watch those stupid teenager shows they have, so I've never seen them, but the dads who've seen them tell me they're filled with the stupidest stereotypes you can imagine. And one of them, of course, is that all band kids are nerds.

Second—as the leader of the Lon Bronson All-Star Band, he kinda has some skin in this whole music game.

"Is your dad a dork?" he said.

"That's different," she told him. "You play trumpet in a rock-and-roll band."

Lon goes, "Well, how do you think I started?"

Alana's adamant—she doesn't want to do it. "I could have easily walked away," Lon told me. "She was in ballet, so that's the art thing. And just because I'm a musician, I'm not going to force her to be a musician—but something kicked in. I didn't like the way she responded."

So Lon brings out his inner Big Daddy. "I think you should give music another try," he says. "You pick an instrument. You try it for one semester. Then, if you don't like it, you can walk away."

This is part of a Big Daddy's job. It's not enough to make your kids happy. Sometimes, you gotta make them strong.

"What I see way too often," Lon says now, years later, "is parents just go, 'Ah, my kid doesn't want to do it. It's kind of a hassle for me to talk 'em into it, so I'm just going to let it go. Especially when it comes to dropping out of stuff.' If you allow your kids to do whatever they wanted, they'd be in front of *Zack and Cody*, 24–7, eating chocolate. You gotta set ground rules. You gotta try to inspire them in some way."

So Lon tells Alana she's in for a semester. Alana figures she's off the hook. Slide through a couple of months in the band, and she's done with it.

Alana picked the flute. And of course, she loved it. And of course, she's great at it. Now she's made the Las Vegas Youth Orchestra, is playing in the high school band, and is practicing enough to drive you nuts.

Which just goes to prove:

Big Daddys are smarter than I look.

Meet My Kid, Pinocchio

The one thing you have to watch out for, once kids start talking, is that you never know what the hell is gonna come out of their mouths.

The other is, they lie a lot.

Not all of them. Just the sneaky ones.

My buddy Felix Rappaport, who was the president of the Mirage in Las Vegas, has two girls. Totally different personalities. The younger one, Briana, is eighteen now, and a real streetwise kid. And she was like that from the get-go. From the moment she learned to talk, she learned the con game: Say anything to get what you want. Apologize later, if necessary. But just keep a straight face at all times.

Case in point: his wife, Mary Louise, is with the kids at Laguna Beach for the weekend. Felix can't make it—he was working that weekend; I think he was at the MGM Grand at the time. Anyway, Louise is with a bunch of friends and decides to go take a walk down the beach, and asks the friends to keep an eye on Briana. She's maybe four or five, and a sociable kid, so she wanders over to a couple at the next blanket over and starts making conversation. Conversation for a five-year-old, anyway, which mostly consists of saying, "Whatcha doin'?" over and over to anybody who'll bite.

"We're just about to go down to the water's edge and look at the tide pools," the woman answers.

"Ooh, can I come with you?" Briana asks.

"Well, you'd better ask your mom first."

"I can't. My mom is taking a walk down the beach."

"Well, then, should you ask your dad?"

Briana doesn't miss a beat. "I can't. My dad is dead."

The couple is stunned. They figure out that Briana's with the people at the next blanket over, so they usher her over there and head for the shoreline. A little while later, the woman comes up to Louise and says, "I'm so sorry for your loss."

"What loss?" Louise asks.

"Briana told us about your husband. We're so sorry."

"Don't worry! He has to work weekends a lot. It's not that big a loss."

The woman is dumbfounded. "He's . . . not dead?"

"Dead? He may be overworked, but it's not gonna kill him!"

Once they sorted it all out, they realized something important about Briana, which is something every dad has to recognize about his daughter if he's gonna make it through: namely, they are born with their own personalities, which are gonna come through no matter what you teach them, and the sooner you figure out what that personality is, the faster you learn to deal with it.

The lesson came in handy for Felix as the kids got older. When Briana was about fifteen, she was with him at a wedding. Felix comes from Philly and happened to know Jon Dorenbos, the long snapper for the Philadelphia Eagles. Philly wedding, big Catholic church, beautiful reception, maybe twenty Philly Eagles are there. Well, Felix knows his daughter really well, and knows three things: One, she loves the Eagles. Two, she's really angry at Michael Vick over the whole dog-fighting thing, which was just erupting at the time. And three, she's not shy about speaking her mind. Sure enough, Vick comes walking into the reception with his entourage, and Felix shoots a look over at her daughter.

She has the look in her eye that a bull has when it sees the big red cape flapping around. She charges, right in Vick's direction, ready to give him a piece of her mind.

Felix, in a move that any linebacker in the place would have been proud of, executes a perfect body block. Suddenly he's nose to nose with his daughter and looks down and says, "You know, there's a time and a place for everything, honey. Maybe this isn't the time and the place for that."

It didn't change her mind, but it did give her a second to stop and think. Just long enough to take the steam out of the situation.

So that's another rule for any Big Daddy. Know your opponent. Even if she is your own daughter.

✦ 4 ✦

WHAT ARE DADS FOR, EXACTLY?

Another thing I was surprised by with my girls is when they discovered sports. Now, I used to think that sports were a guy thing—a guy way of getting ahead, a guy way of showing off, a guy way of being miserable if you're not good at it. But let me tell you, when you have girls, you're not immune. I mean, unlike guys, girls have lots of other ways to wind up being cool. They can even be smart and not get beat up, which was definitely not true in the neighborhood I grew up in. In my neighborhood, the kid who was voted Most Likely to Succeed was also voted Most Likely to Get His Lunch Money Robbed from Him at Recess. Guys, when they're growing up, pretty much have to go through the whole sports thing, and if they stink at all of them, they're pretty much out of the running until they're old enough to start a business and become rich and then make all the guys who were good at sports come work for him, and call him sir, and then fire them.

But just because girls have other ways of dealing with each other as they're growing up—chattering away about who knows what about who said what to who, for example. But sports can still loom pretty large as they round the far corner toward middle school.

And if they're lousy at sports, it can make them as miserable as any guy who ever dropped an easy pop fly with two out and two on.

Luckily, both my girls were pretty good at sports. So we didn't have to suffer much. But my buddy Sammy is another story.

Sammy's kids got into soccer pretty young. I don't know when soccer became the goddamn national sport, by the way. Who the hell played soccer when we were growing up? Okay, sometimes you'd get a kid's math book and kick it to your friends and play keep-away. And sometimes, when we got older, some guys would do that to a certain person's head, if that certain person were to fall behind in his payments on a friendly neighborhood wager on the fifth race at Aqueduct. But that's about as close to soccer as we got. Baseball was big when I was growing up; one, we were in New York, which has the greatest baseball tradition in the country, and two, it played into a thing in my neighborhood that a lot of guys liked to do, which was to whack something with a bat.

So Sammy's kids start playing soccer. At first, it's nothing. Remember that toy we had when we were kids, where there was this bald face on a piece of cardboard with metal shavings around it, and you'd pull a magnet under the cardboard and pull the shavings into place to form a mustache or whatever? Well, that's what a first-grade girl's soccer game looks like. The ball is the magnet, and wherever it goes, this big blob of children follows it around for an hour, and then everybody has a juice box and some Pringles and congratulates themselves on a game well played.

But as they get a little older, some of the kids become "athletes," others are clearly "good team players," and then there are kids who fall into the category of "Look. Everybody can't be good at everything. Have you considered piano lessons?" Those were

Sammy's kids. Sammy told me, "I'd say my older daughter had two left feet, but then at least she'd manage to kick the ball half the time." For the most part, a kid can get sort of lost on a soccer field, and just stay a little outside the action, but every once in a while, just by chance, the ball heads right for your kid, like that extra top left flipper on a pinball machine, and you've got no choice but to watch your kid rear her leg back, take careful aim at the ball, and, with one mighty kick, miss the ball completely and fall flat on her ass.

Charlie Brown would understand, but the rest of the kids on the team, not so much.

In general, it's the dad's job to make sure your kids don't quit at things. Moms are there for nurturing, and telling the kids that sports are not all that important, and gently guiding them to other pursuits. Dads are there for making sure their kids aren't quitters.

But there are limits.

Sammy hit it.

He kept dropping hints that it sure was a long drive to the soccer field, and boy, soccer sure takes up a lot of time, and maybe if somebody didn't want to play soccer that wouldn't be a bad thing. And it all went right over his third-grader's head. Nothing, and I mean nothing, could make her give up on her desire to play every game. Sammy thought, maybe she was just in it for the postgame juice boxes and Pringles. He even went as far as suggesting to his wife that they have that for dinner once in a while. But nothing worked.

It took him three years, three long and painful years, to realize why his kid was so devoted to the sport.

It wasn't the playing, or the hanging out together, and certainly not the satisfaction of scoring a goal, which she had about as much chance of as having Lady Gaga show up at her house and ask her if she was in the mood to go out for pizza.

Nope. Turns out it was something else. Something every dad needs to know about, and be prepared for.

She wasn't participating.

She was collecting.

Turns out, at the end of the year every kid got a medal, and Sammy's daughter decided she really wanted to collect the complete set.

Now, before we get off into this collecting thing, I gotta say one thing. I think this whole business of giving every kid a medal just for showing up has gotten totally out of hand. I understand that the idea is to raise kids' self-esteem. But you know what? Everybody's self-esteem doesn't deserve to be raised for no good goddamn reason. One of my friend's kids, I shit you not, once got a medal at camp for Most Improved Attendance. Look, you gotta reward kids for effort, and you gotta let them know when they're being lazy and give them shit for it, or else how are they gonna learn the difference between working hard and being a lazy fuck?

I think there's a reason to play sports, beyond just having fun (and the whole juice box business), and it's to teach your kids a few things. And the most important one is this:

You gotta make an effort.

So that's the Big Daddy Rule for today: Whatever you do, you give it your best shot. I tell this to kids all the time: I don't care if you're making French fries at the local diner. Try to make the best French fries anyone ever made. I don't care if you're digging ditches or filling them in. Make the effort to get it right.

Look, in the end it's not really about the medals. That's not really what makes kids lazy. You wanna know what makes kids lazy? Dads who don't give a damn.

And here's what makes kids *not* lazy: dads who do.

One of my kids was playing basketball at school for a while. And she came home upset one September, because she sat on the bench for the whole first game. And I told her, what did you expect? You didn't pick up a ball all summer. Did you expect that your game would magically improve even if you didn't touch a basketball for three months? What did you do, sleep with the ball under your pillow and figure that the touch for a jumper would seep into your brain? You didn't make the effort and now you're paying the price for it, which is a good thing, because now you've learned a lesson that a lot of people never learn, which is that you get out of life what you put into it.

Which is not a bad rule either.

Somebody should give me a medal for that.

Hoarders in the House

So, the whole collecting thing. Here's something you can count on, if you are a father of small female persons. If you have daughters, you have hoarders. Plain and simple. Boys can be collectors, too—every guy collected baseball cards, for example, when I was growing up, and when they turned thirty and found out those Mickey Mantle cards they used to have are worth like $500 a pop now, they all lied and said it was their mothers who threw them out. And I knew a kid who collected marbles, although I'm not sure he had all of his.

But for girls, collecting is a religion. I got one friend, his daughter is eight, she collects the following: Barbies. Pokemon cards. Pencils of various colors. Those stupid little metal spoons with the names of the states that you get at airports. Key chains—this kid could be the night watchman at the Plaza Hotel, she's got so many key chains. Snow globes. Shoes. Anything with a picture of Taylor Swift on it. And receipts—why she collects receipts, who the hell knows, but the point is, her parents not only put up with it, they fund the entire project. If the kid ever opens a museum of Crap No One Needs, they can come back and tell me I'm full of shit, but until then, I gotta say: What the hell is wrong with these people? I've seen that hoarders show on television, and the only difference between the folks on that show and my friend's daughter is the square footage of their homes. He lives in a seven-thousand-square-foot mansion on the river, so they have room to store all that junk. If he lived in a two-bedroom ranch, he'd be a prime candidate for that show.

But the real serious problem behind letting your kids get carried away with their little "collections" is this: Every time they see whatever the hell it is they're collecting—a pencil, a key chain, a whatever—they squeal, "I gotta have some!" The parents say, "Okay, but just one," and actually think they're being strict. But the real lesson the kid gets is: Whenever you have any random fucking desire for some random fucking thing, you should indulge it.

This is a really, really bad lesson for later on, when the kid sitting next to them in the dorm has a bong and a bottle of Stoli Vanilla.

The whole collections thing is part of a bigger problem for parents of my generation—because we either grew up in poverty, or we know folks who did. It stands to reason there were rich people in the sixties, of course, but if you're from Bensonhurst, you didn't know them. So what happened was, when we grew up, a lot of guys said, my kid is not gonna live the way I did. She's not gonna want for anything.

Now let me be really honest up front: That's me, on one level. My kids are never going to go hungry. They're never going to go to the grocery store like I did, with a note asking the grocer to front us 'til the first of the month when the check comes in. I'm going to give them the nice apartment, the nice vacation, the nice seats at a basketball game, because I can, and because I don't go a day without thinking, Thank God they don't have to grow up the way we did.

But as soon as I say that, I'll say this, too: If I ever get to the point where I can't say no to my kids, slap me a few times. Because I'll need it.

That's the thing. The "no" thing. There's something in parents today that runs away from the word "no" like they're allergic to it. It just gets under their skin, and they feel like they have to give their children what they want.

It's all because they don't want to be like their parents. Their parents were strict, so they don't wanna be like them. Which to me is first-degree bullshit.

Look, I'm not gonna do something as important as raising my daughters based only on doing the opposite of whatever somebody else did. Because the opposite of chaos isn't order—it's just a different kind of chaos. You gotta have a plan for raising your kids and the plan can't be just, I'm not gonna do what my parents did.

Think about it in terms of what you do for a living. For me, learning to be an actor wasn't just about watching bad actors and doing what they didn't do. I don't care who you are—if you're a stockbroker, you're not gonna get rich by watching bad stock brokers and just not buying the stocks they bought. You're gonna do well by watching good stockbrokers and copying them.

For me, I copy guys like my friend Pete. I mean, he's nothing like me—this guy has never raised his voice in his life. I've usually raised mine twice by the time I brush my teeth (usually once to say, where's the goddamn toothpaste, and two, to argue that wherever the hell it is isn't where it was yesterday. I don't find anything wrong with yelling in the morning. Clears the head and gets the day off on the right foot. Also wakes the kids and saves me a trip to their room).

But one thing Pete does is he says no. Often. I was with him having a drink in his den one time, and his kid came in and asked for something—I can't remember what it was, maybe to go over to a friend's house, and Pete says no. When the kid left the room, I asked Pete why he said no.

Pete smiled, took a pull on his Scotch rocks, and said, "Practice."

Pete also solved the collection problem. I said it was mostly a girl thing, but I guess not, because his nine-year-old son was a hoarder of the first order.

The idea started one Christmas. Pete was trying to figure out what to get his son, who was asking for a ton of shit. The kid actually came back from a family trip that Thanksgiving with a *Sky Mall* magazine from the airplane and was circling everything he wanted (which included a stuffed golden retriever the size of a Winnebago, a set of toy zombies, a tent, a teddy bear with a hidden tape recorder inside so you can get it to say whatever you want—including, I guess, "Buy me more shit from this catalog"— a remote-control monkey, a pair of military night-vision binoculars, and a bunch of other crap—what kid needs fireplace tongs I don't know, but apparently he thought they were cool).

So here's what Pete did. He came up to New York in the beginning of December, and he gave his kid fifty bucks, cash, and set him loose in FAO Schwartz. "Whatever you want, buddy—one thing for fifty bucks, fifty things for a dollar, you decide."

The kid was really happy. And he really got into it: For the first time in his life, he's picking up toys and looking for the price tag. Pete had given him a little notepad and pencil to carry around, and he's down on the floor next to the plush toys, adding up his take so far, trying to decide if that cute little lion is actually $49.95 cute, or whether the smaller one has a better cuteness-to-dollar ratio.

They all came home happy. After that, he put the kid on a budget for all his collectibles: You can have ten dollars a month for all the little crap you collect. You decide what's worth it. Suddenly, he's in a store and going nuts over some crappy toy, and Pete says, you can have it, and starts to take it to the register. And the kid goes, wait—if I get that, how much do I have left for the month?

And *that's* the lesson you want them to go to college with.

It won't solve the whole bong and Stoli thing, but it's a start.

The Bottom Line

And let me say one more thing about money. When you're trying to teach your kids the value of a dollar, you also gotta teach them: That value only goes so far.

When it comes to my girls, all I want is to raise them to be good people, and I want them to be safe. That's it. You ask me my philosophy? That's it. Not complicated. I don't need them to be brain surgeons. I don't need them to make a lot of money. I don't judge people by how much money they make, because in my business you meet a lot of assholes that I can't stand who are really wealthy. You give me a garbageman and a rich asshole, I'm gonna go have a beer with the garbageman. It would be nice if my girls find a way to make a living. But that's not what's important to me. I want them to understand what's important in life. I'm happy I'm able to give them what I can give them. I wish I could give them more.

You see these rich rotten trust-fund kids around Manhattan, going to the clubs, strutting around like turkeys that got a pardon on Thanksgiving. Which makes me sick. But it's not the money that pisses me off—it's the fact that no one taught them that with money or without, what makes you a decent person is how you treat other people. Not what you have—what you do. These rich guys who give all their money away because they want their kids to have to struggle so they'll understand the value of a dollar—I don't get that. That's stupid to me. What, my kids have to go on food stamps to appreciate life? But the opposite—the guys who make it big and set it up so their kids don't have to lift a fucking finger—that's ten times worse.

Look, I've been lucky up to this point. But I'm a fifty-five-year-old fat actor. I've had a good run for the last thirteen years. But I never know what's gonna happen. I don't take anything for granted. And I make that clear to my kids. They need to know that you never take anything for granted. So we don't live too large or too extravagantly. My daughters go out to dinner, they go to the diner. They don't go to some $100-a-dinner joint. They know they have to contribute, so they babysit in the building, and one of them has an iPhone that she paid for with her own money. The other has an iPod, same deal.

Do I really need them to work? Financially, no. But do I need them to work so they understand that what they get doesn't fall from trees? Absolutely. Look, I don't want them to worry when they go out with another family, like I did when I was a kid—I'd go out with some friends' parents and sweat the whole time thinking, are they gonna pay for me? I'd squirm and worry because I didn't know what to order, and didn't have enough to pay for myself. So I don't want them to ever, for one second, feel like that. But at the same time, I don't want them to walk around with no regard for money. I don't want them ordering the most expensive lobster or the most expensive steak because they don't understand the value of a buck.

So I'm not gonna ever put them in the position I was in when I was a kid. But I'm also not gonna indulge their every whim, either. My oldest one doesn't drive; Ciara, when the time comes, is gonna get a car. But she's not gonna get a Corvette. See, this is a lesson I taught them from the time they were little. I was a maître d'. I came home with my pockets stuffed with cash. I would take them out and say, "Come on, let's go buy stuff." But they learned early on, this is not something to take for granted.

Because in the end, what it's about is teaching them that the stuff isn't what's gonna make you happy.

Treating people with respect is what's gonna make you happy. Because then they're gonna respect you back.

And how do you learn to treat people with respect?

Easy. Practice on your dad. And don't worry, if you step outta line, I'll be the first to let you know. Free. No charge.

And before I get back to the whole "no" question, I wanna say, there's one more way to teach your kids to treat people with respect. And it's the most important.

You gotta treat your wife with respect.

I argue with Laura all the time. Hey, I argue with everyone all the time. But I don't think I've ever, for one second, treated her with anything but respect. And I think that's the best lesson I ever taught my kids. Nothing I said to them—not that I don't say some brilliant things, I gotta admit—but nothing I ever said to them is as important as just letting them see how I treat my wife. How I listen when she talks. How I say thank you when she cooks dinner. How I apologize on those rare situations when I'm wrong.

Because I think my kids get that. And I think that now that they're starting to hang around with boys, they'll make some better choices. I think they've learned to expect that kind of treatment from men, and they won't hang around with bums—God willing—because they've learned to expect that. You gotta show your kids that bad behavior is not acceptable, and the only way to show them is to show them.

Look, of all my fears—and it should be clear by now, I have a shitload of them—one of the biggest is that one of my girls is gonna wind up with some asshole who doesn't treat her right. Or I should say, that was one of my biggest fears. Like I said, now that they're starting to date boys, other than giving me a heart attack that they're actually dating, I'm starting to see that they are making decent choices. That the guys are not jerks.

That's a big load off a Big Daddy's mind.

So far, anyway.

Screen Pass: Taking a Pass on Screens

I'll tell you one more thing that I said "no" to a lot when my kids were little.

Too much TV.

Hey, I know I make my living from TV, but in general I didn't like them watching it all the time.

When Bria was small, *Rugrats* was a big show. But one of the main characters, Angelica, was really mean and nasty. So what does Bria do? She starts imitating Angelica. Trying to act mean and nasty. Like I don't have enough troubles in my life, I need a TV show to teach my kid how to act like a snotty bitch. So we cut that off.

But we let them watch some TV. You gotta. You can't cut them off from the world altogether. She liked *Barney* a lot. I know it's cool to make fun of *Barney*, but you know what? It was sweet, and she loved it, and so I got no problem with that.

I'll tell you what I do have a problem with. Video games. We never let our kids get anywhere near them. Because I think they make you brain-dead. I know these adults who play them constantly; I know every NBA player supposedly plays video games. I don't care. I think they're asinine. I know there's all kinds, but the violent ones are the worst. Like Grand Theft Auto. I find it absolutely horrible.

But even if they're not horrible, they're mesmerizing, and they make kids not want to get out of the house. That's one thing my mother had right on the nose—Saturday morning. Come on! Get up! Let's go! Out of the house! We'd go to a movie, or go bowling, or whatever. But these kids with the video games—they sit there for hours. You look at them, they have the face you see in zombie movies. I think they have the cast in the zombie movies play video games before the camera rolls, just to get in character. And the parents don't give a fuck because it's what the parents want—"As long as the kid is quiet and out of my hair, I don't care what they're doing." And that continues through life: If the parent says, "As long as they're not causing me a problem, that's fine," then you get into that mentality.

And then you really have a problem.

Look, I know we're all busy. You're working, your wife is working, you have no time for yourself. I get it. But just shove a kid in the corner with a video game—that's not a solution. That's a recipe for disaster. Next thing you know, the kid is out playing Grand Theft Auto, only it isn't a game. And there's no reset button on life.

More Great Moments in Big Daddy History

I gotta tell one more story about my friend Lon, because this, to me, is another one of those things that explains exactly what a Big Daddy is about.

Lon's got a kind of home office in the back of his house. It has a separate door to the outside. I know a lot of you think of Vegas as the strip, but Lon's like I was. He lives in a nice suburban neighborhood, old-growth tree-lined streets and all. You kind of let your guard down when you live in a place like that.

Until you don't.

One day, Lon's working in his office, looks up, and there's this total stranger standing there, staring at him. Breathing heavy, like he's been running. Odd-looking guy—wiry, shaved head. And at the same instant, Lon realizes he's hearing police sirens in the neighborhood. And they're close by.

This, Lon thinks, is adding up in a way that is not good.

He challenges the guy. "Who the fuck are you?" he yells.

"Please, you gotta help me!" the kid responds.

This is not an option.

Now, if the kids were not in the house, Lon says, he knows he could have run out the other door, found the cops, and let them deal with it. But he knows his kids are home. And that's the last thing he knows. Everything after that happens by instinct.

"I don't know what happened," Lon says. "He could have had a gun, a knife, anything. All I know is, I charged the guy. It wasn't like I made a conscious decision."

Lon and the kid start struggling. "I'm fifty-two and I'm not in great shape," Lon says. "This guy is very young and big and wiry, much stronger. But I'm just so charged with adrenaline. I rushed at him and pushed him out the door. I've got him in a bear hug, and I'm screaming for the police."

Lon gets the guy back out the door. Now he has the guy's arms pinned and is trying to push him into the pool. He figures if he can get him in there, he can immobilize him. The kid spins, and his shirt rips, and the next thing Lon knows he's got a fistful of shirt and the kid is running for a seven-foot retaining wall. Lon grabs a pool skimmer, and as the kid vaults the wall, he's beating the kid with the business end of the pole.

Lon doesn't know it, but his wife has heard what's going on. She's gotten the girls out the front door at this point and flagged down the cops. She's yelling at them, "He's got him! He's in the back!"

The cops burst through just as the kid makes it over the wall. They catch him in the next yard. Turns out he had a felony conviction, was being chased by the cops, ditched a stolen car two streets over, and had run into Lon's office totally by random chance.

Lon says he doesn't know what came over him, in that moment, when he was confronting a stranger with his kids in the house.

I know what came over him.

What came over him is what's inside every father, especially every father of girls. It's the pure animal instinct to protect your daughter. At any cost. There's no thinking. There's no deciding. There's no nothing. When the instant comes, you just do what you gotta do. And fuck anyone who threatens my kid.

That, my friends, is as good a motto for a Big Daddy as you're gonna get.

✦ 5 ✦

MOMS VS. DADS

'm not much of a football guy; I'm more a Yankees fan, and then a baseball fan, and then a Knicks fan, and then a whole lot of other stuff, and then maybe a nap and a good meal, some red wine maybe, and then football. But I know a lot of guys think of life as a football game. And they think they're the quarterback in their own house—making key decisions, directing the offense, marching the team down the field. Or maybe the coach, calling in plays from the sidelines, keeping the running game and the passing game in balance—are we eating in or out? Should the kids go to camp this summer or stay home? One big gift for Christmas or a lot of little ones? He thinks of himself as the field general who marshals the troops and keeps the game flowing. Dads are surprised that no one dumps Gatorade on our heads more often.

But actually, when you come right down to it, I think of myself and my wife more like officials than players or coaches. And the difference is pretty obvious: My wife is an umpire. I'm a referee.

Umpires are the judges of things no one else could possibly

judge. Did that eighty-five-mile-an-hour slider cut under the midpoint between the batter's armpit and his belt just before it crossed the front of the plate, or just after? Give me a fucking break. I could do that job equally well with my eyes open and with my eyes closed, which is to say, there's no way. They're the ones making hair-tight calls between safe and out, between fair and foul, between the ball that tipped the top of the wall as it went over and the one that didn't, which they can tell with pretty damn good accuracy, even though they're a hundred feet away. You know how good they are because every time an instant replay shows they blew a big call, it's on Sports Center within ten milliseconds, and you don't see them that often. Baseball is a game of inches, and umpires are the rulers.

Referees, on the other hand, are a bunch of zebras running around amid twenty-two lunatics in war paint and helmets, re-enacting the battle scenes from old cowboy-and-Indian movies sixty to seventy times an afternoon. Only most of the football players don't have guns or bows and arrows (although I'm not so sure about the New Orleans Saints).

Approximately 99 percent of what goes on around the referee goes unnoticed. You'd have to have eyes in the front, back, and sides of your head to see every time somebody pushed, shoved, held, tickled, goosed, or wedgied somebody, kicked them in the groin, or stole their last cookie. (Okay, some of those are football things, and some of those are kid things. I get a little confused sometimes. So sue me.)

My point is, moms are like umpires. They make all the tiny little decisions of the day. The arguments that moms get into with their kids are incredible to me. They can argue over the tiniest stuff. How much is too much to spend on fingernail polish? Which dress is too dressy for school? Which one's not dressy enough for church? One friend of mine goes to church every Sunday with the family, and he says that half the morning is spent with the mom sending the two daughters back upstairs to change their clothes, and he swears that they come down in the exact same dresses, only now the mom says, that's fine, let's go. No way he could tell the difference. No way he could tell a slider from a split-fingered fastball either.

Dads, on the other hand, are the referees. We ignore about 90 percent of the bullshit that goes on around us. We have to: It's all noise and chaos to us. Especially dads who have three or four kids: Saturday morning is a complaint-fest. He poked me, she started it, he's hogging the milk, she took the last Froot Loops, it's my turn to pick the channel on the TV, no you picked it yesterday, and on and on and on. If dads tried to be umpires, and called every one of those plays, they'd go crazy.

But like referees, dads—good dads, anyway—Big Daddys— know when to jump in. I was over at this friend's house, a guy who has four kids, and it's like insanity. We're having a beer, we're watching the ball game, and there's this little ongoing war around him. All the kids have some complaint with each other. I don't think he's paying attention to any of it. Then, out of nowhere, he spins. "Joey! Give him back that ball! That's his!" "Trey! You poke her like that again you're in a lot of trouble!" "Andy! Intentional grounding! Fifteen yards and loss of down!"

So that's what a Big Daddy is. A lot of what goes on around us we don't give a shit about. But just let someone think they can get away with something on our watch. Fifteen yards.

Overall, it all works out pretty well in our house. We wind up splitting the discipline up.

Like I said, Laura handles more of the minute-to-minute decisions, and I step in when I see a flagrant foul. But in a lot of families I know, it's usually one or the other who's calling the shots. It can go either way.

My buddy Mitch Modell, who is the president and CEO of the family's Modell's Sporting Goods, is the first one to admit—

his wife is in charge of the discipline. He's in charge of screwing it up.

"My wife is a real disciplinarian, which I guess she learned from her mother," Mitch told me. "She keeps the kids on track. I'm the easy one. With me there are no rules. With my wife, it's only rules. My boys, when we go to a game or when my wife's out of town, they say the best thing is, 'Dad, there are no rules with you.' We make up the rules. I deprogram them, and my wife has to program them again."

Hey. Whatever works.

Get Your Wife a T-Shirt That Says "No" (As Long as She Takes It Off Before She Gets in Bed)

I wanna say something else about how moms and dads—or how moms and Big Daddys—argue. A lot of the guys I know have the same complaint.

Remember before I was talking about how important it is for dads to learn the word "no"?

Apparently it's ten times harder for moms.

If moms are the umpires, then they tend to be the biggest pushover umpires in the league. Any ballplayer who argued a call as much as kids get away with arguing with their moms would get thrown out of the game in two seconds.

Moms may try to make all the decisions, but they haven't figured out how to throw a kid out of a game. It's like I was saying before, about learning to tell your kids, "Do it because I said so, end of story." If you don't learn how to end an argument, you're screwed.

One dad I know told me, "If last night in my house was a sitcom, the line in the *TV Guide* would be, 'Mom tries to get the kids to bed. Hilarity ensues.'"

He says that just about every night, Mom tries to get the kids to turn off the TV and go to bed, and every night they say, "Please, just one more show," and these are the responses he'd heard in just the last couple of weeks:

—"Well, only if you eat your cereal while you're watching."

—"Okay, but this is the last time."

—"Why, what's on?"

—"But aren't you going in to school early tomorrow?" (To which the kid says, "Pleeeeease!"—which the mom finds to be a pretty decent argument.)

—"Honey, you'll get too tired, and I don't want you to be tired for your test." (To which the kid replies, "Pleeeeease!" "Pleeeeease!"—which the mom finds to be an even more decent argument.)

And so on. Another dad I know told me his wife and daughter can do fifteen minutes on whether she can have a little more ice cream. And that negotiating a sleepover at his house took longer than negotiating NAFTA.

So what do the dads do, other than pulling their hair out?

The Big Daddys step in—like a referee. Not on every instance, only when it gets serious. The dad whose wife can't get the kids to bed every now and then will step into the room and say, "I think I heard your mother say turn off the TV."

And the TV goes off.

Why?

Because now you are the bully on the playground. But it is a good thing here. I promise.

At some point, it doesn't hurt to go a little crazy on everybody. Some good ranting and raving and yelling and screaming, and dealing out punishments like a hand of cards.

Once you do that, you shouldn't have to do it anymore. Just like the bully on the playground—he hit somebody once, and now nobody messes with him. I'm not saying you gotta be a bully in your own house—far from it—but I am saying that once in a while, Big Daddy has to show everybody what's acceptable and what's not.

Every now and then, I'll hear Laura and one of the girls going at it. Laura's telling her to do something—turn off the TV or change her clothes or whatever—and the argument is going back and forth and back and forth like a windshield wiper with no off switch.

I'm the off switch.

"Did you hear your mother?" I'll yell. "I heard her and I'm in the next room. How did you not hear her? She told you to turn off the TV. Why is that TV still on? I don't get it. Can somebody explain this to me?"

Do I sound a little pissed off to you?

Good. Because I am. And there's not one thing wrong with that.

And guess what? I don't have to do that very often.

Just once in a while. To make sure nobody forgets.

Let's Make a Deal—the Home Version

I do what I do because I know: If you have girls, you have negotiators. My buddy Hugh Fink is a funny guy. He does great stand-up, and now he's got a new show on Nick Jr. called *Parental Discretion*, where they talk about this stuff.

One of the things they're gonna talk about on the new show, Hugh told me, are the so-called new parenting rules. Among these new rules, he said, is one called "specific praise."

"Like if you kid paints something, instead of saying 'That's pretty,' you're supposed to say, 'I really like the way you mixed the blue and the green.'

"The trouble is," he said, "it's exhausting to try to find so many ways to say something specific and positive. Like, my kid is playing softball, and she strikes out. What am I supposed to say, 'I really respect the way you saw the ball coming and swung and missed again—it shows your persistence'?"

Yeah, like I got a lot of patience with the new parenting rules. Me, I like the old ones just fine. And one of the most important is: No negotiation.

Hugh has two daughters, one ten and one seven—and from the start, he says, everything's a negotiation. "It's like having a Persian rug dealer in the house," he says. "Honey, I need you to brush your teeth and go to bed." "Okay, I brush my teeth and go to bed . . . if I get to watch one more *Barney*. Please, please, one more *Barney*." "Okay, you can watch one *Barney*, but then go to bed." "Tell you what I'm going to do for you, Daddy. I will brush and floss . . . if I get two *Barneys* and three yogurt pops! Take it, Daddy, it's a good deal. Take it! Take it!"

Now, when it comes to the negotiating thing, dads can be as bad as moms. And if you think your younger kids are good at negotiating, just wait. When it comes time for them to start going out, it's gonna become an every-night thing. That's why you need the Big Daddy rules.

There's this one buddy of mine, told me what it's like when his teenager goes out at night, and I don't wanna embarrass him, but I gotta say, who's in control here? The dad or the kid?

Girl says, I'm going out.

Dad says, Where you going?

Going out with my friends.

What time are you coming home?

I'm coming home at eleven.

No, that's too late. Be home by nine thirty.

Everyone else is home by eleven.

I want you to be home at nine thirty.

C'mon, Dad, how about ten?

I want you to be home at nine thirty.

But why? Why can't I come home at ten?

Okay, you can come home at ten.

How about ten fifteen?

Here's what the dad could have said.

He could have said, "I said nine thirty. I'm not just telling you nine thirty because I pulled it out of my ass. I'm not doing it to spite you. I'm not doing it because I like that number. I'm doing it because I think eleven o'clock is too late for a fourteen-year-old girl to be out there. That's why."

Yours truly, Big Daddy.

Tell you the truth, we don't have this problem too much in my house. My wife is pretty strict. It's just that I'm a lot stricter. Too strict, sometimes. Like when they want to go to a party. Why do they have to go to a party? I'll ask. What, they don't see these kids enough all day at school, she can't wait twelve hours to see them tomorrow? What do we have to do, have an intervention for her friend-addiction?

And my wife will explain to me, patiently, that based on her many years' experience, the fact of the matter is, I am being a total jerk.

So, there's a good argument. I can respect that.

But like I said, respect is what it's all about.

This whole negotiating thing, the whole talking-back thing— it makes my teeth hurt when I hear it. That's gotta be the main rule you carry away from all this—that the kids have to respect you. They have to. No two ways about it.

I hear how some of my kids' friends talk to their parents. Especially to their mothers. And I have no problem being the guy who says, not in my house you don't. I have no problem not being the cool parent. I have no problem being the strict parent. I relish the chance to be the Big Daddy.

It's like I said before—I'm not shy about saying, you see the life you live here? Do you want it to stop? 'Cause it'll all stop. You want to go to a fancy private school? You know what? You can go to public school with everybody else. Maybe it'll be okay, maybe it won't. I don't know but we'll take that chance.

I mean, I don't want to say I threaten my kids. But I guess there's an implied threat. And there has to be. And you know what?

My kids don't step out of line.

I think that making sure your kids talk to you with respect is important in every family, but it's especially important in families that are well-off. Because those, I have to say, can be the most obnoxious kids around.

I know a lot of guys who are doing pretty well. When you're in the TV business, you're around people who've done okay for themselves. I've been lucky that all the kid actors I've worked with—every one of them, from *The Sopranos* to *Secret Life* to *Nicky Deuce*—have all had a pretty good head on their shoulders. They're not stuck-up, they're not full of themselves. They have teachers to homeschool them on set, and they do their work, and they're respectful to the people around them, to the crew and to the fans and all.

Which is great, because nothing pisses me off more than seeing some well-off kid acting like he's hot shit. I have one friend who's a millionaire a lot of times over. And he treats his kids really well—they have the chauffeur, the fancy vacations, the whole shebang. But if this kid acts high and mighty one time—if he snubs a waiter, or if he disses some other kid for his crummy clothes or whatever—the dad comes down on him hard. And I mean hard.

"Who the hell do you think you are?" I heard him tell his kid once, when he caught his kid acting snooty to another kid at school. "What exactly did you do so far to earn what you've got? What you did was get born into this family. Well, guess what. Everybody you know got born into their family. That makes you exactly tied with everybody else when it comes to having actually done anything. Now go apologize."

That's Big Daddy talking, right there.

My Daughter the Star

Now, when I say all the kid actors I've known have been pretty decent kids, I gotta take a minute to add, I wish I could say the same about the parents. Not the parents of the kids on my shows, thank God—but there are some parents in my business who have their heads so far up their asses, they should charge themselves for a colonoscopy.

The thing of it is—and the lesson that parents who aren't showbiz parents should listen to—is that they push the kids too hard. All the time. Do this, do that, go to this ballpark and sing the national anthem, go over to that table and say hello to that director who's trying to eat his meal in peace. Go to this audition. That one. Another. And then when the kid manages to get a part, they're all over the director—don't present my kid this way, my kid shouldn't be saying that line, whatever. It gets to the point where they poison the whole business for the kid, because no one wants to deal with the crazy parent. The parents are trying to live through the kid, trying to get the kid to be something the parent never got to be.

Which happens all over the place, and not just in show business, by the way. So watch yourself.

Still More Great Moments in Big Daddy History

But it's an issue we all face—if we're lucky. We grew up poor and learned some tough life lessons from growing up poor. Now we want to make sure our kids grow up having the things we didn't have. But how do we square that with making sure they learn the same lessons, and not grow up to be, not to put too fine a point on it, well-off spoiled douche bags?

My buddy Felix, who was the president of the Mirage, has his head on pretty straight about it. He grew up with a single mom doing her best to raise two kids in Philly. "She bought me a corduroy coat at a fire sale once," Felix said. "It was an actual fire sale. I smelled like barbecue for two years." Felix's wife also had a single mom, and just like Felix, she grew up without a lot of money. So now that they're doing well, how do they teach their kids what's important?

Felix says it's all about figuring out what values you want them to learn and looking for excuses to drive those lessons home. Example: His older daughter, Alexandra, was driving herself to school when she was sixteen, and ninety-nine times out of a hundred she was running late and in a hurry to back the car out of the garage. So, she's backing the car out of the garage, like she always does, and ninety-nine times out of a hundred it's okay because there's no one behind her.

This one time out of a hundred, unfortunately, the cleaning lady, Rosa, is parked behind her, and Alex proceeds to drive smack into Rosa's car. After which she immediately runs into the bushes to hide.

She pulls out her cell phone and calls her mother and tells her what happened. The mother asks her where she is.

"In the bushes," she says. "I can't face Rosa."

Now, I would have used this as an opportunity to release some steam into the atmosphere, say, maybe, enough to inflate a hot-air balloon and fly it to Cleveland. Felix, being of the small group of fathers I like to refer to as "sane," chose instead to make it a moment for learning. The mom calls him and tells him what happened. When he gets home, he has a talk with Alex. A much calmer talk than I would have had.

He told Alex that he wasn't disappointed in her for crashing the car; he was disappointed in her for hiding from Rosa. Because facing up to your mistakes is more important than whether you make them. Everybody makes mistakes; not everyone knows what to do about them. Now you know.

See, maybe my friend Felix and I talk about this stuff differently—like, maybe I talk about it a little louder—but it's all about saying to your kids, "Look, the street smarts I had to learn the hard way, you get to learn the easy way. I had to learn them to survive; but you get to learn them to be a better person. And they're not that complicated." People think "street smarts" is about learning to con people, but it's really just the opposite. Street-smart guys know that con men get caught and go nowhere, eventually. Really street-smart guys know that what you put out is what you get back. So the rules are simple—and they're the rules that Felix teaches his kids.

Felix's rules for his kids are: Fess up to your mistakes. Make good decisions. Be honest. Be ethical. Treat people the right way. Choose your close friends wisely. Don't surround yourself with negative people.

And find things in life you really love.

See, I can go along with that. Maybe not as calmly as Felix, but as long as you get the point across.

How Many Moms Can a Man Get Pissed Off At, Before You Call Him a Man?

Now when we're talking about the difference between moms and dads, it's important to remember that there's a lot of ways it breaks down.

Because there's lots of different kinds of moms and dads.

And if you haven't guessed by now, most of them piss me off to no end.

Let's start with the moms.

First off, there's the Control Freak mom. These are the ones who have to be in charge of everything. Dads have to fight to even be heard in a house like this. From the get-go, everything the dad does is wrong. It's because moms like this need to feel like they're in control. This guy Scotty I know, he says his wife is like that. (Scotty's not his real name, of course. He wanted to use his real name, but he said his wife wouldn't let him. She said she didn't want people to think she was bossy, and that was the end of the discussion. My heart goes out to Scotty.) He said it started when their daughters were just toddlers—he tried to get in there and be an involved dad, but whatever he did, she could do it better, and she made no bones about letting him know it. Like dressing the kids. When Scotty was in charge, his kid apparently always left the house (according to his wife) in clothes that were: Too Warm, Too Cold, Too Small, Too Big, Too Dressy, Not Dressy Enough, Mismatched, Wrong for This Particular Occasion, and, once (he swears this is true), Too Green.

A lot of moms are like this. My buddy Hugh Fink says dealing with his wife is like going up in front of a federal prosecutor. "She'll break me down," he says. "I'll bring my daughter home from a party, and it'll be, like:

'How was the party?'

'It went well.'

'Did Claire *eat*?'

'Yes, she ate.'

'Well, *what* did she eat?'

'Oh, you know, they were serving hot dogs and stuff.'

'Well, did she take her lactose medicine?'

'No, she didn't.'

'She *didn't*? Oh, *really*. Did she complain about her stomach at the party?'

'No, she didn't complain.'

'Well, have you asked her how she felt since the party?'

"It's sort of like there should be a court stenographer," Hugh said, "I'm just waiting to be arrested for something that I did or didn't do."

On the opposite end is the Pushover Mom. This is the mom whose kids know exactly where her buttons are and how to push them. Watching a mom like this with her kids is like watching the Muppets—you see the mom's mouth and arms moving, but you know somebody else is actually in control. Only in this case, the person in control is a lot younger than Jim Henson was, and not nearly as funny.

A close relative of hers is the mom who the kids always make fun of. This is another thing that drives me crazy. I see it all the time. Whatever the mom says, the kids roll their eyes and make a sarcastic remark. I think it's terrible—here's Mom cooking, cleaning, scrambling, doing every conceivable thing for the kids, and they make fun of her. They're a bunch of little shits, if you ask me, but it's the fault of the moms, too, because they put up with it.

When I hear a kid talking to a mom like that, I always wanna walk up to the kid and say, you know, you think you're so smart. Let's see you run the house for a day. Go deal with the laundry and the shopping and getting everybody to school and to soccer practice, go figure out how to pay the bills and get the guy to come fix the broken toilet, go call the doctor and figure out why your little sister is coughing, and then while you're at it go change a few dozen diapers that smell like the downwind side of the garbage dump outside a cheap Chinese restaurant. And just for good measure, let's see you give it a try while some snot-nosed kid is heckling you from the sidelines, telling you you're doing it all wrong.

You know, if the acting thing doesn't work out for me, maybe

I'll hire myself out as a consultant for moms like that. Could be a good gig. Might not pay real well, but man, that would be satisfying work. I might even do it as a volunteer in my spare time.

And then there's the Needy Mom. This is the one who is always trying to please everybody. Her kids are even bigger snots than the pushover mom's kids because they know their mother will do anything to make them happy. This is a dangerous weapon to put in the hands of a child.

There's also the Muscle Mom—for some reason I feel like I know a lot of those—the moms who spend the whole day at the gym. They may not know the name of their kid's science teacher, but they can bench their weight and have biceps the size of casaba melons.

There's the Superefficient Mom, of course. She's the expert scheduler. The planner. The one who's a step ahead of everybody. She's the one with the charts on the refrigerator with exactly where everybody needs to be for the next six months. She's the one who divides the chores up like a drill sergeant; everybody in the house knows who's doing the dishes a week from Thursday. In her spare time she helps the air traffic controllers figure out better landing patterns at JFK.

She can be okay, although usually she's a major pain in the ass.

Then you have the Guilt Mom. Constantly making you feel guilty about whatever. And her twin sister, the Poor Me Mom. She's the Look At What Your Father Did To Me Mom. Constantly complaining. I can't stand that. I remember one girl who lived in the building told my wife, "If I could just drink a glass of wine alone. That is all I want." To me, I think, "What are you talking about? I mean really? What did you become a mother for, so you could complain about your kids? So you could whine about how tough things are for you? My heart bleeds. Get a fucking clue."

Then there's the mom whose kids can do no wrong. No matter

what happens, it's somebody else's fault. The teacher screwed him over, the coach screwed him over, this one doesn't like my kid, that one has it in for my kid. You know what you're teaching that child? You're teaching that child that you don't take responsibility for what happens to you. That kid's gonna need a lot of help when he grows up. Or a lot of therapy.

My favorite mom—as you might guess—is the Tough Love Mom. This is the mom who takes no shit from anyone (dad included). I always think of this one woman who lived near a friend of mine in the Bronx as the classic Tough Love mom. Her name was Mrs. Grataglia, and she lived on the first floor of an apartment building on his block. She would spend the day hanging out the window, yelling at every kid within earshot—and with her voice that went a long way. "Jimmy! Put that down." "Joey! You let your brother have that ball." "Tony! Give that boy back his pants, I'll smack your face."

Mrs. Grataglia lives on today in the moms I see around our neighborhood whose kids are the most polite when you meet them. I swear to God, when one of the girls comes home with a friend, and the kid is nice and polite and looks you in the eye when they meet you, I know already I'm gonna like the mom.

I could go on—there are a whole lot of different kinds of moms out there. Mothers are complicated people. But dads are a lot simpler. There's just a few kinds of dads.

I'm not talking about the lunatic dads—the ones who put the Scotch in the kid's milk to calm him down—or the asshole dads, the ones who mostly aren't there, and when they are you wish they weren't.

Putting them aside, there's basically three kinds of dads: The Golden Retriever, The Gym Teacher, and the Big Daddy.

As you probably guessed by now, two of those piss me off.

Anybody who's ever had a golden retriever will tell you they're the easiest dogs to train. They're smart enough, they're friendly, and they're basically happy to be told what to do. Lots of dads are like that. Just tell me where to go, what time to be there, what to wear, what to eat, what to say, whatever. These are guys whose mothers put their clothes out for them until they were sixteen, guys who brought their laundry home from college, guys who did what their moms told them to do, and now that they're married, they're happy to have the wife take over that role. You want me to go to the grocery store? Okay. Let me get my shoes. You don't want me to order the steak? Okay. Can I have the fish? Fine. You don't want me to go play poker on Thursday night? Okay. Can I watch the baseball game? Good.

Guys like this are harmless enough, I guess. But they're basically parents who aren't really parents. They're sitting there in the kitchen, eating their fiber cereal, and watching the world go on around them, wondering if they should pipe up about anything, then thinking better of it and just keeping their yaps shut. They've got the parenting skills of a sofa cushion.

The Gym Teacher dad is just the opposite. This is the guy who was born with a whistle around his neck. These guys live by the philosophy that if you tire your kids out enough, they won't cause you any trouble. There's one guy we know, when the kids were getting a little rambunctious, he made them go out and do laps.

Around the block.

When they were six.

These are the guys who go out and coach their kids' Little League teams and get a little too intense about it. The ones whose kids play every sport in every season, whose kids are hiking in the woods with them at six in the morning when any self-respecting father is telling everybody to shut up because it's way too early to be talking. I'm sure their kids do just fine in life.

They're too scared not to.

The Big Daddy is somewhere in between. It's all a matter of balance. You gotta let the players play the game. You gotta let them slack off a little bit in the second half. And if it looks like things are getting out of hand, that's when you bring the hammer down. Not too often. Just often enough to let everybody know you're there.

A lot of people are going to read this and say, okay, you're talking about going back to the fathers of our parents' generation, strong and tough and all that, right?

No, not right. That's not the definition of a Big Daddy. And I'll tell you why.

Look, the dads of our parents' generation had it tough. I'm not talking about my dad, the star of the movie *The Man Who Wasn't There*. I'm talking about the vast majority of families, where the dad worked hard, he came home, he watched some TV. The mom had the kids, the dad had the living room.

The dads weren't expected to get all that involved in homework, in child rearing, in any of that.

What kids need—what kids have always needed, but especially today, with all the shit they're exposed to and all the temptation around them—is a dad who is more than willing to get involved. In everything. And most important, willing to get involved when the kid is starting to screw up—willing to look the kid in the eye and say, "What you are doing, this does not make me happy."

And to stand his ground until the kid realizes that this is not a good situation to be in and that it's in his best interest to make it right. And fast. When he makes his dad happy, then he gets to be happy, too, which is a good thing all around.

That's what a Big Daddy does.

Got it?

Good.

That makes me happy.

6

BIG DADDY JOBS

'll tell you one thing I did with my kids that I think is an important job for a Big Daddy. Because I know a lot of guys who don't do this. And I think it's a really important part of being the father of young girls.

Starting when they're about five, and ending just about never, you gotta teach your daughter to throw.

With boys, it's a natural—every father dreams of it. They make movies about it. The whole point of *Field of Dreams*, every guy's favorite baseball movie (even though it has a lot less sex in it than *Bull Durham* and isn't as funny as *Major League*), is that Kevin Costner has to go through all sorts of shit because he never had a catch with his father, and at the end he gets to, and they act like that's the most important moment in the history of the universe.

Which it is.

Having a catch with your son connects you to something that runs very deep in every guy. It's an image of days gone by, of auld lang syne. It connects you to Ruth and Gehrig and DiMaggio, and

Tinkers to Evers to Chance. Every guy hums "Take Me Out to the Ball Game" to himself when he's having a catch with his son, and he thinks, "I don't care if I never get back." It's the only activity you'll ever do with your kid where he gets tired of it before you do. The lifelong bond between a father and son is formed in the shape of a lazy arc of a ball lobbed softly on a summer afternoon.

But a girl?

Doesn't happen. Should, but doesn't.

Guys do not have this image with their daughters. A lot of the guys I know never had a single catch with their daughter. I mean, they tossed a big bouncy-ball around when they were two, but having an actual catch with an actual ball and glove? No way.

The bond that you want to have with your kid—the bond that makes it possible to yell and scream and do all the things you need to do to keep them in line, for their own good—that bond is formed not in any big way. It's formed in ten thousand little ways.

And ten thousand throws is a good way to start.

I heard someone tell me once about something called the "ten-thousand-hour rule." It's the idea that people get great at things through repetition—a lot of it. The reason the Beatles were so good, for example, is all those years they spent playing ten-hour gigs at clubs in Germany.

Now, I don't really get the math here, I mean, ten thousand hours is a lotta hours. But it's the idea of it that works with your kid—if you say, I'm just gonna do this, all the time, over and over, until she's good at it, then a couple of things will happen.

One is, she'll get good at it.

Two is, it'll help her build confidence—doing anything that well is gonna give you confidence—and that goes way, way beyond throwing a baseball.

It also means that if some kid is giving her shit, she can hit them with a rock pretty well, which also gives you a certain amount of confidence. Not that you should teach your daughter to hit people with a rock, unless they really deserve it. But I'm just saying.

But on top of that, there's something else that's gonna happen.

And that is, you're gonna spend hours together, not talking, not arguing, not doing anything but tossing that ball back and forth. And one toss at a time, like a spider spinning a gigantic web between you out of fibers so thin you can't even see them, tossing that ball across that distance between you is gonna change that distance between you.

It's gonna make it smaller.

And believe me, as they get older, that's pretty damned important.

And don't get me wrong. This is not about trying to turn your daughter into the son you never had. I told you, the minute I heard I was having a daughter, I was delighted. I was relieved. And I never for one second felt any different. I don't wish I had a son. I mean, I wonder about it sometimes. But being the father of two incredible daughters is the greatest pleasure I've ever had in my life, other than finding a woman to marry who would put up with a guy like me. You don't teach your daughter to throw because you want her to be like a boy. You teach your daughter to throw because it's good for her, and it's good for you, and it's good for the both of you together.

And it's not about trying to make girls and boys be the same, either. I got friends like that. There was this one couple we knew when the girls were little, real nice hippie couple, they decided to raise their kids in what they called a "nonsexist" way. They gave dolls to the boy, they gave toy trucks to the girl. They dressed them identically in OshKosh B'gosh overalls and little denim shirts. They censored every book that came into the house to make sure it didn't have stereotypes of boys and girls. They didn't give the girl anything pink, and they didn't give the boy anything blue. I mean, they were dead serious about this.

So what happens? Girl goes off to preschool. Comes back the first day, I shit you not, announces she wants to be a ballerina when she grows up. Parents have a fit. But don't you want to be a truck driver? How about a congressperson?

Who asks a kid if she wants to be a congressperson? Give me a fucking break. The kid doesn't fall for any of it. She starts throwing a tantrum. She wants to be a ballerina. She starts doing that four-year-old ballet thing girls do, spinning around and falling on her butt.

Parents finally give in. Buy the kid a goddamn pink tutu. Kid wears nothing else for a month.

Good for you, kid. For all the torture that little girls are going to have to go through, not being a girl shouldn't be one of them.

On the Road Again

One of the things that's hard for a lot of dads is that they have to travel a lot. This is especially true in my profession, because when you're an actor, you go where the work is, and if that's Timbuktu, then you're going to Timbuktu (unless they happen to be subbing Van Nuys for Timbuktu, in which case you're lucky. They can do so much with CGI these days). Tim Van Patten, who directed a lot of episodes of *The Sopranos* and is now the executive producer of *Boardwalk Empire*, had a unique solution to that: He'd pull his kids out of school and take them on location with him. It meant they had a lot of homeschooling (and let me tell you, these kids are smart as a whip). It also meant that when he was in Australia shooting HBO's *Pacific*, his kids were in Australia exploring the jungle, holding koala bears, swimming in gorges, and chasing wild kangaroos. There's a lot of different kinds of education in the world.

When I traveled with my kids, it was more for fun than for

work. I think by the time Bria was five years old, she had been in Hawaii six times. And my kids were pretty easy to travel with. But I will say this: When you're traveling with little kids, it's amazing how much shit you have to carry. The car seat. The diaper bag. The emergency medical kit. Ten tons of clothes. The toy bag. The stuffed animals. Sixteen different kinds of food because goddamn if any two kids ever eat the same thing. Another buddy from *The Sopranos*, Michael Imperioli, went on vacation with us once to Jamaica. He had three kids, I had two. We had so much stuff with us, we looked like the Jews crossing the desert after they left Egypt. I felt like we should sit down and have a Passover seder right there at JFK International. "Until the kids are about five years old," Michael used to say, "you're basically a mule."

Like any dad, I had to go off and work sometimes, and miss time with my kids because of it, but I will tell you this: When I was home, I was really home. And my wife was home. We spent our time with the kids because that's what we wanted to do, and you know what? It paid off, because later, they were used to it and they wanted to spend time with us. This guy I know has a friend with a nine-year-old kid, sends the kid to sleepaway camp for nine weeks. Who the hell does that? What, you want someone else raising your kids for you? Are you too lazy or busy or just too full of yourself to do it? Get the fuck outta here.

I see it all the time, in my neighborhood. You walk around downtown Manhattan in the afternoon, and you'll see it: All the nannies with the kids. Four or five nannies, standing around talking, six or seven kids playing nearby. Look, some households, both parents gotta work. Especially today. It's not like when we were growing up and you could get by on one parent's salary. I get that. Some guy's making thirty grand a year and his wife has to take a job, and he's gotta take a second job—they're doing what they gotta do for their kids, and I love that and I respect that.

But come on. My neighborhood? I'll bet there isn't one family in ten that they're both working because they gotta work. They're both working because they feel like it, because it makes them both feel more important; or they're both working because they just wanna be able to get more shit. And if you got a coin, do me a favor and flip it to help me figure out which of those is more stupid.

You're working to survive, to pay off the mortgage, to afford a car, okay, I get it. You're working for those other reasons, you know what, stay the fuck home and raise your kids. Don't let somebody else do it for you.

Maybe some people aren't cut out to be parents. I mean, they like having the kids around, sometimes, so they feel like they're living a full life—but when it comes to the nitty-gritty of dealing with their moods and tempers and needs, and feeding them and carting them around, and all that other shit—they can't be bothered. You hear these horror stories from parents—Oh, my kids, they're driving me crazy, My wife is so stressed, I can't take it—well you know what? Suck it up. You had the kids and they're yours and if you don't like the way it's going, then man up and make it better.

I was at this one family's house, I swear to God, the kids are running around like lunatics, and the mom is yelling, "Shut up! I hate you!" Who yells that at a kid? What kid is not gonna become a lunatic if the mother is yelling "I hate you"?

So these parents, they go out, they both get jobs, and they hand the kids off to the nanny. And if that doesn't suck big time, then I don't know what does.

And here's the flip side. So let's say both parents are working, for whatever reason. They see the kids for maybe thirty minutes in the morning, when everybody's running around trying to get out of the house, and they see the kids for a couple of hours at the end of the day, when it's mostly homework and showers and stuff like that.

So when they come home on the weekend, they wanna have a good time with their kids. They wanna have fun with them and show the kids what great parents they are.

So they don't discipline their kids for shit.

The kids are brats, because the parents don't want to punish them in the few hours they're spending together. And the reason they don't want to spend more time with their kids is, the kids are brats.

You gotta figure out a way out of that cycle, ladies and gentlemen.

Because the nanny sure as shit isn't gonna figure it out for you.

Ballet, and Other Forms of Big Daddy Torture

When you are home, and you do make the commitment to spend as much time as possible with your kids, your world starts changing in all sorts of ways that you didn't expect if you have a couple of girls in the house.

Like, for example, going to the ballet.

Now, look, I know there are some boys who are into the ballet. And good for them. One of the dads I talked to takes his son to the ballet once a year.

On purpose.

But for the most part, ballet is a girl thing. Like I said, when you have a couple of girls in the house, sooner or later someone's gonna notice that the ballet is next month, and someone's gonna get tickets. Which is perfectly fine.

Except for one thing.

I hate the fucking ballet.

So I'm not the one to talk, here.

But my friend Dave says it's not so tough, if you prepare

correctly: Go online and read a review of a previous performance, so you understand what the hell is going on; maybe find a video of this particular troupe, so you know what to expect; and fill a large hip flask with Ketel One Vodka.

This is not, of course, the only way to prepare for a ballet, Dave says.

Absolut is also perfectly acceptable.

Once you've been dragged, moaning and groaning, to the ballet, he says, you might as well accept that you're there. Watch the graceful dancing, listen to the music.

And take time to consider the fact that these are the most flat-chested women you've ever seen in your life.

Admit it—any guy who's ever been to the ballet (read: every guy with daughters, or every guy trying to impress his date with how cultured he is, which is not my idea of how to get laid—I mean, some things are just not worth it, but to each his own), that's the first thing he notices.

Before he elevates his consciousness to the finer points of ballet.

Like, for a bunch of flat-chested women, they have some pretty great butts.

Don't give me a hard time for this. I've been to strip clubs where the outfits are less revealing than the stuff people dance ballet in these days.

I don't get the ballet at all. For one thing, all the women are always dancing on their toes. This makes no sense to me. Why don't they just get slightly taller women and save everybody the trouble? And the guys keep picking the women up and holding them above their heads, and the audience breaks into a huge round of applause. What's the big deal? These women look like they might weigh a little more than a Thanksgiving turkey, and with a lot less meat on their bones. How big a fucking deal is it that this guy has lifted her over his head? Come on. You wanna get guys to come to the ballet, let's see him clean and jerk one of those big fat opera singers. I'd pay good money to see that one. I mean, go up a weight class or two. It might do good for your career. If Sugar Ray Leonard could do it, so can you, that's what I say.

But while you won't have the slightest idea of what's going on onstage, you can be glad for the fact that at least it doesn't last for three hours, except, of course, for the fact that it does.

Which brings us to the most important point in appreciating the ballet: Sit next to your wife, so when you start snoring she can give you a sharp elbow to the ribs and wake you up.

So why, if the ballet is so fucking boring (except for the cute butt thing), should the father for any reason accompany the family to the ballet? Why not save 150 bucks for the extra ticket, send the family off to the Opera House, and sit back with a cold beer and a Knicks game and congratulate yourself on a well-organized life?

Dave's reason is this.

When the ballet is over, and his daughters and his wife are babbling on about how wonderful it was, and he's just glad the damn thing is over with, he piles everyone in the car. The little one falls asleep on the way home because it's way, way past her bedtime. And Dave carries her up the stairs, and lays her down on her bed, and she half wakes up, and he asks her, "Did you like the ballet?" And she says, "It was the best ballet ever." And somehow, in that very moment, she knows that Mom went because Mom loves the ballet, but Dad went because he loves his daughter.

And that, Dave says, is why you go to the ballet.

Big Daddy Rule for the Day: Be Prepared, and Be There

But like I said, not me. You'd have to have my balls in a vise grip to get me to go, and even then I'd try to make a break for it.

But I do make sure that I find things that my kids and I can do together. Lots of things. I love spending time with my kids. And I'm lucky because they like spending time with me. Because in the long run, that's all that matters.

You know why that's all that matters? Because time flies. Let the family go off without you once too often, and before you know it, you're going to be squeezing into a tux that doesn't quite fit you anymore, and you're gonna find yourself standing in the back of a church with your little girl holding your arm, preparing for the shortest walk of your life, at the end of which she will kiss you on the cheek, and turn to look at a guy who fits into his tux a lot better than you do into yours, and the expression on her face will change, in a way you've never seen before.

And the next time you see her will be when the moving men come to take her boxes down from her room, boxes filled with one of two things: memories of days you spent together, or memories of days you didn't. And which boxes they are carrying will make all the difference in the world, at that moment.

To her.

And to you.

I have this photographer friend of mine. He told me that the philosophy of news photographers—the secret to getting the greatest photos—is, be prepared, and be there. If you're jumping out of a car and the firefighter's running out of the burning building carrying the dog in his arms, you don't want to get caught with your pants down. Make sure your camera's batteries are charged, and make sure you have a spare. Make sure your lens cap is off. The "be there" part, of course, is that if you don't get to the fire in time, the dog will already have been rescued and all you'll get is a shot of the other photographers congratulating one another over the fantastic photo they just took and you didn't.

Be prepared, and be there. Good rule for photographers. I think it's a great rule for dads, too.

For one thing, you always have to be ready. Ready for anything. That's the dad motto. We may be useless a lot of the time, but when the call comes in the middle of the night that your darling daughter has a flat tire on Route 9, or the kid who's supposed to drive her home had two more drinks than he promised, or someone left the gate open and the dog escaped and someone has to drive the neighborhood in the pouring rain with the windows open, hanging his head out the window and yelling "Fluffy" over and over and fuck the neighbors if it wakes them up, then it's Big Daddy time.

So dads always have to be ready. That's what comes naturally.

What comes less naturally is the other part. The "be there" part.

Here is my advice to you on that:

Suck it up.

Just go.

Go to the ballet, to the stupid animated movie, to the soccer game. Whenever you can, be the one to pick her up from the birthday party, from the playdate, from the movie. Look, you're working, and you're gonna miss a whole lot of stuff. Half a lifetime's worth of stuff, when you think about it. So don't be a lazy jerk and miss the other half. I know a guy who used to have a "daddy day" with the kids on Saturday—all the dads took the little girls someplace, ice skating or the museum or something—and his philosophy was, Now that I put in my time, I get time off tomorrow so I can watch the Jets.

Here's what I say.

I love sports. I especially love the Yankees and the Knicks, and when your girls are old enough, and if you're lucky like me, you can get them to watch the games with you. But you know what? They're girls. They're gonna be interested in stuff that you are not.

Suck it up.

Be there.

Because you only get one shot at this.

Your Life Is Holding on Line Two

When it comes to getting his daughters interested in sports, you would have thought my buddy Mitch, the Modell's Sporting Goods guy, would have had that under control. He's a dad of five kids, and his two oldest—they're in their twenties now—he tried everything to get them into sports. But it just didn't take. Some girls—and I guess some guys, too—just won't go there. It was pretty frustrating for him, to tell you the truth. He's making up for it with his younger kids—two boys and a seventeen-year-old girl. They're all sports kids.

But I'll tell you what Mitch does have down: the whole idea of being there. Being a big, present, there-when-you-need and there-when-you-don't kind of dad.

"I work my schedule around my kids," Mitch told me. "My daughter's volleyball games, or soccer games, baseball games—I try to attend every one of them. When I'm on the sidelines, I know—they're always looking over to see if I'm there."

I was surprised, when Mitch told me that; I mean, this is a guy with a lot of responsibility. He's a very busy guy.

But he doesn't let himself get too busy for his kids. "Believe me, it's tough. It's not easy," he said. "But like anything else. God forbid you get a call and a friend passes away and you have to go to a funeral, you always seem to manage to show up. That's how I treat their schedule. Like everything is that important."

The funny thing is, his kids don't realize how unusual that is. How guys like Mitch and me, who didn't grow up with a dad who did that sort of thing, know how unusual it is. The kids don't get that. But you know what? Kids never do.

"They don't understand it," Mitch told me. "But I never understood it until I had kids. I only wish my father had gone to my basketball games or baseball games. He went to one baseball game my entire life. In Little League. You see other parents there, other fathers there, you know, you kind of accepted it. But when I look back, I would never want to leave that kind of void in my kids' lives."

One of the reasons Mitch is like that, I think, is that he's an older dad. Like my buddy Anson Williams who I was telling you about before—when you're older, your priorities change. Mitch doesn't care how anybody looks at him in a meeting—and I guess, maybe when you're the boss, you don't have to care—but when his kids call, whether it's the young ones or the grown ones, everything stops and he takes the call.

Hello? Big Daddy speaking. Can I help you?

Big Daddy Alarm Clock

You know who else is great at being there? Joe Piscopo. I told you earlier how he spoils his kids rotten. But he's a great dad. I love this guy. He's lots of fun. He was like a lot of us—balls to the wall with his career, back when he was on *Saturday Night Live* in the early '80s. But he got a wake-up call like you wouldn't believe.

In 1981, he was diagnosed with thyroid cancer.

"That kind of smacked me in the face," he said. "It was when I was at *Saturday Night Live*. It scared the hell out of you. 'Cancer? What?' So that drew me to focus on my family and my children, more than anything. 'Oh, got it. You could die.' And if you die, nobody gives a shit if you were a celebrity. The only one who cares is your children."

So Joe started taking his little son on the road with him. As his kids got older, he kept it up.

"I'm busier now than I was then," he told me. "So I make it a point to take the kids with me when I go to shows. I have a big show next Thursday up in north Jersey. I'll take the kids. I'll take them to school in the morning, I'll take them home. I'll bring them to the show. I'll put them backstage, I'll put security on them, they'll do their homework, they'll hang, I'll bring them onstage. I've done this for years."

I'll tell you something else he's done for years. He's taken care of his kids. Joe's divorced, but he has the kids half the time, Sunday through Wednesday, and sometimes more than that. But he doesn't have a nanny or anyone taking care of the kids for him. He's in there himself, being a Big Daddy. He does the laundry, he makes the lunches, he cleans the freaking toilet. Everything.

A lot of guys in his position would have a lot of help. I asked him why he doesn't. Typical Joe, he joked about it: "All my money goes to my ex-wife. I want to save a little for myself. Plus, my record with running off with nannies is not a great one. That's my problem. My mother keeps saying. 'Joseph, you better get a seventy-year-old nanny.'"

But bullshit aside, he doesn't have a nanny because he knows it's about Being There.

"I want them to know how involved their father is, number one," he told me. "Let my children see me doing all the housework and making all the lunches and the snacks and helping with the homework—it builds character with the kids, and that's why I do it. This is why I was put on this earth.

"They are my life," he said. "I am dedicated to my children. I don't have any personal relationships, my career suffers, but it all pales in comparison to giving your life to a child. I should have been a woman. I have the motherly instinct. I can look in their eyes and see if they have a fever. I should be wearing a housedress. Not a pretty thought, I know. I'm like a dad savant. The rest of life is like a mystery to me, but I feel very comfortable with being a father."

Amen to that, brother. Amen to that.

My Weekend Daddy Is a Dickhead

A lot of the divorced dads I know, they're not like Joe.

Not to put too fine a point on it, a lot of divorced dads are dicks.

The problems is, they see their kids on the weekends, maybe. If that. And when they do, they wanna be the happy guy—they just wanna show the kid a good time. They don't want to discipline their kid on the one day of the week they get to be together.

In other words, they don't want to be a dad.

It's like a version of the guy who goes out with his mistress. He sees her once a week, they stay in the great hotel, he buys her gifts. They don't argue, they don't fight. Every day is Christmas Eve. Everything's wonderful. That's why a guy has a mistress. It's Fantasyland.

The divorced dad is the same way. He just wants everything to be wonderful. Especially if the divorce was his fault. Now he knows the mom is saying all sorts of bad shit about him all week, and he's got one day to clean up his reputation. So suddenly he's Santa Claus. Brings the kid over, they're going to dinner, to the game, to the park, they're gonna pack a week's worth of stuff into a day and a half. Because he doesn't want to feel like he's missing out on anything.

Problem is, he's missing out on everything. He's missing out on nagging them to write their homework neater, to not wear their skirt so short, to watch their language, to clear their plate after dinner, and wash a pot or two while you're at it.

He's missing out on being a dad.

But I'll tell you what I really don't like with divorced dads—or divorced moms, either. It's when they bring the new boyfriend or girlfriend along when they have the kid.

You see the kid little enough. The one day she's with you, you gotta bring the girlfriend around? You know, unless it's serious, unless you're saying, "I'm gonna live with this woman, so you should get to know her"—until that point, what is the reason for screwing these kids up? Either they're gonna get attached to this woman who then you're gonna break up with, so they get messed up again just like when you left, or else you're gonna show them that life is about screwing some woman and then moving on to the next one, which is a really great lesson for a teenage girl just crashing into puberty head-on.

And on top of all that, you lose any ability you have to control your kid at all. You can't discipline a kid if they don't respect you. And what teenage girl is gonna respect her mother or her father if they're gonna go screwing around like an idiot?

Now I know a lot of times the divorce is the dad's fault. Because he was cheating. Look, it happens. I'm not gonna preach about it. That's not what I'm about. I just will say, for me, that I can't imagine it. I mean, what, just to get laid, you're going to screw up your whole life, and your kids' lives, and everybody's life? Why? There is nothing I can imagine that's worse—nothing—than imagining somebody else living in my house. Some guy, sitting down to dinner with my wife, my kids. I'd slit my throat first. Why would you take a chance on that happening? Just to get laid?

I actually know fathers with grown sons, and they're both cheating on their wives. So the father is with his gumare at a restaurant, and he runs into his son. And the son is with his gumare, too. The two of them, sneaking out to a restaurant in Jersey with their mistresses, and they run into each other! How does that conversation go? "Don't tell your mother." "Don't tell my wife." Very odd. But that goes on, and we know that. I just can't imagine taking the chance. Some guys like to gamble. To me, the risk is just too great.

This one guy I know, I'll leave his name out of it, but he was a big shot in the Democratic Party, and he got to meet Bill Clinton a couple of times, and one time he brought his daughter. This was after the whole Monica Lewinsky thing, and the guy's daughter is the same age as Chelsea, and Clinton asks the guy, "Does she still hold your hand in public?" And the guy says, "Well, of course she does." And Clinton gets this sad look on his face, that kind of sad smile he has, and he says, "Chelsea won't hold my hand anymore."

I'd feel sorry for Clinton if he hadn't been so stupid. But like I said, I'm not gonna preach about it—that's not my place. I just gotta say, for me, when I look at my friend who cheated on his wife and got kicked out of the house—I think, you got your whole life ahead of you with your family, and there's not a whole lot you can do to fuck it up. It's pretty easy to figure out what you need to do to hold it together, and if a guy's too much of an idiot to figure that out, then he's got enough problems without me telling him what an idiot he is. So I'll just leave it at that.

(But really. Guy throws it all away just to get laid? What an idiot.)

7

GROWING UP

I'll tell you one other thing that didn't happen in my house as the kids got older. The kids did not take control. I told you before that we started this when the kids were little, the idea that the grown-ups are in charge. This gets harder as they get older. And it also gets more important. In my house the grown-ups still get to be the grown-ups, and the kids still get to be the kids, and we kind of leave it like that. It works for everybody and it keeps me from blowing my top.

Which is exactly what I want to do when I see how this friend of mine lets his kids take over his life.

I won't say his name, of course, because nobody who is this much of a pushover as a dad needs to be embarrassed in public. I mean, maybe he does need to be embarrassed in public, but I'm not gonna do it, and I don't know if it would do any good anyway. He's been at it too long.

I was working in L.A., and this friend of mine and his daughter were in town visiting, and we hung around for a few days. And I'm telling you, a few days is about all I could take.

Every five minutes, the dad is checking with the kid on what we're gonna do next. Do you want to go back to the hotel? Should we go back to the hotel? Do you want to watch TV now? Do you want to eat in or eat out? Where should we go? Chinese? Would you like Chinese? No? Sushi? No, you don't want sushi?

How about I just lie facedown in the street, you take my wallet, hail a cab, tell him where we're going, and I'll just ride in the trunk? That's what I'm waiting for the guy to say.

I mean, the kid is a nice kid. Just turned thirteen. She's not a whiner, she's not a complainer—but she doesn't have to be. The guy is checking her pulse every five minutes to see if she's the least bit unhappy with anything that's going on in the universe. And the worst thing is she doesn't give him a clue—she doesn't ask, "Dad, can we please go out for steaks tonight?" He's there playing Kreskin, trying to read her mind, and she's just saying, "No. Guess again." It drives me fucking crazy.

In my house, I'm in charge, and there's nothing wrong with that. I'm not a dictator. I'm not unreasonable. Except for when I am. But I mean, I'll give the kids choices, sometimes. And sometimes I won't. A lot of the time, it's, "We're going out to dinner tonight, this is the restaurant we're going to, this is what you should wear." Am I gonna tell them what to order? No. But am I gonna let them overrule the grown-ups and decide where we eat, when we eat, what we eat? No fucking way.

It's not that I'm a selfish guy. I would do anything for my kids. I would give them the moon if I had a ladder high enough. But I won't fuck them up by making them think that the moon revolves around them. For one thing, I think as a grown-up you get to make the decisions. And for another, I think that as a teenager, you have to know that you don't.

Splitters

There are other ways I see people's kids taking control of the house that drive me nuts. One is a term for some kids that Laura and I use—we call them "splitters." My mom was a person like that—she liked to split people up. She played one kid against the other. She'd tell you something that your brother or sister said about you, whether it was true or not. She'd do it all the time. Divide and conquer, maybe that was her strategy. Whatever it was, it was screwed up. Anytime she saw two of her kids getting too close to each other, she'd find a way to drive a wedge between them. Try to make you jealous, or pissed off, or something. This didn't even end when we moved out—she kept it up. So now everybody's wires are crossed, everybody's fighting with each other, and she's the kingpin.

But nowadays, when I see splitters, it's not the parents. It's the kids. They play one parent off the other. "Hey, Dad, when you were out of the house, you know what Mom did?" "Hey, Mom, you told me I can't do this, but Dad already said I could."

My kids never pulled that shit. Because they knew they'd never get away with it. Maybe a couple of times, I'd tell them it's time for bed, and they'd say, "Mom told me I could stay up later." I'd be the fucking district attorney on this. Oh, your mother said that? Are you sure your mother said that? Well, let me call Laura Schirripa to the witness stand. Mrs. Schirripa, did there come a time when you told your daughter she could stay up late? No? Thank you. You may step down. Bria Schirripa, would you please take the stand so I can hold you in contempt of court and tell you what's gonna happen if you ever pull a stunt like that again?

I rest my case.

Now, Ladies and Gentlemen, Put Your Hands Together for . . . Big Daddy!

But don't get me wrong. Being a Big Daddy isn't always about bringing the hammer down. Far from it. In fact, as the kids get older, one of the dad's most important jobs is stand-up comic. Let's face it, life can get pretty serious if you let it. And you can't let it. And dads can be the ones who make it too serious. I can have a shit fit if one of the kids fucking curses in front of me, and no, the irony in that sentence doesn't escape me for a moment, so shut the fuck up.

My point is, even though it's dads who can raise the temperature in the house, it's the dad's job to lower it, too. Like I said earlier, we got born with that Three Stooges gene (which, by the way, is the real difference between having boys and having girls. Males are born loving the Three Stooges. I'm yet to meet a woman of any age who says, "Yes, I find their humor fascinating." It just doesn't happen. For any guy, "Nyuk nyuk nyuk!" is the funniest sound in the world, unless it's maybe the sound of Moe getting whacked in the face with a two-by-four, or knocking Curley in the head with a hammer. Now that's comedy).

For those of us in show business, we have a natural sense of pride in being performers. But every dad is a performer with his kids. It's just a matter of what you bring to the stage with you. As I mentioned, my buddy Tim Van Patten directed a lot of episodes of *The Sopranos*, so when his girls were little, he'd get down on the floor with them and their Barbies, and make up stories, which happened to be Sopranos plot lines. "This is the good Barbie," he'd say, "and this is Barbie the Rat. Barbie the Rat stole Ken's car. So now good Barbie is out looking for her. Good Barbie has to whack Bad Barbie. Look! She found her! Now she's going to whack her! Whack! Whack! Whack!"

Okay, so they don't need to know exactly what "whack" comes to mean at a later date. You get my point.

My other buddy from *The Sopranos*, Michael Imperioli, used *The Simpsons*. He and his kids bonded over *The Simpsons*, and you go over to their house for dinner and they're always quoting lines from that show. Nothing cracks them up like when Michael quotes his favorite Homer Simpson line: Whenever any of the kids piss him off, he stands up, tosses down his napkin, and says with all mock seriousness, "You people have all stood in my way for long enough—I'm going to clown college!"

You use whatever you have to entertain the kids. Me, I liked to just do whatever outrageous thing came to mind—like when the Jerry Lewis telethon would come on. I'd call up to make a pledge, and I'd say to the woman taking the call, "We're seeing you guys on TV right now. I'll pledge an extra fifty bucks if you scratch your nose this second." The woman on TV would scratch her nose, and the kids would fall on the floor laughing. (Okay, may not sound that funny to you, but hey—you gotta know your audience. With five-year-olds, the nose joke kills.)

Every dad has some kind of funny thing—every good dad, anyway—some kind of game or running gag going with his kids. It's part of the glue that holds you together. You know, when you're having dinner together, sometimes the conversation with a kid takes a little work. "How was your day, honey?" "Good." "What happened in school?" "Nothing." "Didn't you have a test?" "Yeah." "How did you do?" "Fine." It's like having a conversation with that Magic 8 Ball toy we used to play with. "Are you doing okay in math?" "Ask Again Later."

So one of my buddies uses the time to play word games with

his kids. It gets the conversation going, and after a little while, they forget that as preteenagers it's their job to be silent little shits.

When they were little, he used to play the last-letter game with them. We knew this as geography—I say a state or a country or something, like Arkansas, and you say a city or country that starts with an S, like Seattle, and so on. Only with little kids, once you get through America, the city they live in, and Oz, you've pretty much used up all the place-names that they know. So he assigned everybody at the table various degrees of difficulty: The six-year-old could say any word she thought of. The mom, who worked in a restaurant, had to use names of foods. And the dad, who worked in film, had to use only movies with one-word titles.

This is all nuts, if you ask me. But it worked for them. His son came up with a good answer, and they're all high-fiving around the table beaming, like he was the guy who drove in the winning run in the World Series.

And it's not even time for dessert.

This lawyer I know, William Arnone, he and his daughter had a whole bunch of things he calls "rituals." One of them is, they used to read *Harry Potter* together, and act out every chapter. Then, when the movies come out, they go to see them to see whether the actors used the same kinds of voices they did. It's family legend that the daughter did Haggard the Giant exactly the way they did it in the movies. The kid is off to college now, but she still calls her dad and talks about how great this was. They also were Abba freaks—big dancing parties in the bedroom, screaming out the lyrics to "Dancing Queen." And another one—this one is nuts, to me, but if it works for you, it works—is, every Sunday, they'd get *The New York Times* and read the names out loud from the wedding section. As often as not, something would crack them up. Like, they'd find a Judy Smith marrying a guy named Anthony Pazutti—"She's gonna be Judy Pazutti!" his daughter would scream.

They did this every Sunday, without fail. Now, that's love.

Big Daddy Rule: No Such Thing as Quality Time

For those of you who say, aren't all these games just a way of not talking about anything important at the dinner table, and isn't that time for discussing the issues that your child is facing and putting in the quality time with your children, to this I have a very simple response.

Go fuck yourself.

Because here's the secret. Here's the one that nobody gets. Here's the lie that parents tell themselves to excuse the fact that everybody's working and the kid is being raised by the nanny.

The secret is this:

There is no such thing as quality time.

There is only quantity time.

Raising kids is not a sprint. It's a marathon. You're not the psychiatrist, and the kid sits down at the table for fifty minutes, and you have to get to the root of their problem. Because more likely than not, the fact that you have so little time for your kids *is* the problem. Look, I've been honest through this whole book, and said that when my kids were young I was working and traveling a lot. I can't say I regret it—you know, I was building a life, I was doing what I was doing for them as much as for me—but like I said, when I was home, I was home. I was right there. I spent as much time with my kids as possible.

And the whole point of spending time with your kids—which is where that whole have-dinner-as-a-family thing comes from—is about giving them a chance to bond with you. To let their guard down, to just hang around and be their stupid selves. And for you to be your stupid self.

And be honest: Sometimes, it just gets boring to talk about the goddamn math test and the homework and what this teacher said to that kid. Sometimes, you gotta amuse the kids just to amuse yourself.

One writer I know in L.A., his dad was a failed vaudeville comic. The dad was always telling his bad jokes to his kids. They all involved some guy named Schwartz—"Schwartz falls out a window. Guy runs up, says, 'Schwartz, what happened?' Schwartz says, 'I don't know, I just got here.'" Swear to God, you talk to this writer, and he idolizes his dad. Father never made twenty grand a year, but you listen to the guy and you'd think he was goddamn Milton Berle. Gives his dad credit for him becoming a writer. Now he tells all those stupid jokes to his daughter at the dinner table.

Sounds like a form of child abuse to me, right? But his kid loves them. The stupider, the better. He says he feels like it ties the generations together—I mean, he's told his kid all the stories of his family history, coming here from Germany to escape the Nazis, all that—but the thing that he thinks bonds the kid to that history, more than anything else, is that schmuck Schwartz. And who am I to say no.

Telling dumb jokes is one of those things that the daddy-kid bond is built out of. Like having a catch. And listen: When they get older, and you really need them to trust you enough to tell them the important stuff—like whether there was booze at that party last night—you're relying on that bond being there. Because you don't want to try to find out whether anybody was drinking and driving, and hear, "Ask again later."

Discussing Loudly

Not all dads are comedians, of course. Some of the guys you'd think would be real cutups around the house turn out to be the most strict. A good friend of mine, Joe Medeiros, was the head writer of *The Tonight Show with Jay Leno* for sixteen years. This guy could make a joke out of anything. But as a dad, he was all business.

In fact, around his house, he had the reputation of being the guy who was always angry. When his daughter was little, he was more of the reverse-psychology kind of guy—he'd ask her to come to her room and put on her pajamas, she'd say "no" and run away, he'd say, "Okay, don't come here. I don't want you in this room. Stay away." And of course, she'd come.

"She never listened," Joe said. "She was a great kid, but I knew she was a little unusual, because she crawled on her head. She would flip over on her back, arch her back, and crawl across the floor that way. So I knew she was a little different."

But as she got older, her tendency to do things her own way got under Joe's skin. "I had a hair-trigger temper," he said. His daughter wouldn't do her schoolwork, no matter what he and his wife did. "I'd tell her fifty times," Joe said. "Then finally I'd throw a fit. I'd yell and scream, and then I'd let my wife come and clean up after."

This, to me, is a great plan. It's how we won World War II. The dad is the air force, coming in and doing the carpet bombing; Mom is the infantry, coming in after, going door-to-door and taking prisoners, while Dad's already back at the base having a beer and congratulating himself on another successful mission.

See, Joe's like me. He comes from an Italian background— even though his dad was born in Hawaii, of Portuguese descent. But his mom's Italian, and he grew up in Philly, and Sundays at

Mom's house were a spaghetti-and-screaming fest. The football game would be on the TV, and the relatives would all be yelling— they'd yell at each other, they'd yell at the quarterback of the Eagles, they'd yell at each other for yelling at the quarterback. "It was never, 'Come here sweetie,' 'Sit down darling,'" Joe said. "It was always, 'Comere! Siddown! Eat! Now!'" Joe told me they never called it yelling. "We preferred, 'Discussing loudly.'"

And see, I get that. You can't let the kids run the show. By the time they're grown up, you want them to have a voice in their head, telling them not to do the wrong thing. Hopefully that will be a loud voice. And hopefully it'll sound something like you.

There Is No Such Day as Independence Day

When girls turn into teenagers, they suddenly think they're going to start getting more freedom. They want to act more independent, and they want you to let them act more independent.

I tried that.

Once.

I took Bria out to Los Angeles to the Screen Actors Guild awards. Laura didn't want to go, so she stayed home with Ciara, and it was just me and Bria. She was about twelve years old at the time. So we go out to dinner at Dan Tana's with Michael Imperioli and Seymour Cassel, another buddy of mine, great character actor, used to be in all the John Cassavetes movies. Bria is great— she's not one of these kids who you have to give them the little video games or DVD players or comic books in a restaurant. She'll talk to people, she'll take part in the conversation, she'll make eye contact. That's important to me.

We were staying at the Peninsula, one of the nicest hotels in the country, and it was early. So me and Michael and Seymour decide to go have a drink at the bar, and Bria says she wants to stay in the room by herself. And I decide, well, she's old enough for that. I tell her about twenty times, just stay in the room in the bed and watch TV. Don't leave this room for anything. Don't answer the door for anybody. ANYBODY. Also, stay in the room. And what if someone comes to the door? Do you let them in? No. Just stay in the room. Lock the door from the inside. I show her how to lock the extra lock they have on hotel doors. And I go over the whole thing again. We reach "Daaaaaaaad"—that point kids get to when you're really driving them nuts.

So then I only tell her two more times. And I go have a drink with the boys.

I leave her in the bed, watching TV, and I'm gone maybe twenty minutes, and I go back, and I try to get in, and I can't. Good girl, I think. She locked the door from the inside. So I knock, and I call her name.

No answer.

Shit.

I knock again, harder. I call her name. Louder. Nothing. I'm panicked like I've never been panicked before. Every fucking thing you can imagine happening, I'm imagining. She hit her head. She fell in the bathtub. Somebody got in the room. I'm dying.

I call the hotel security, and they're there in two seconds, and I tell them what's going on. They take the latch off the door, and the security guy turns to me, and says, "Do you want me to go in first?"

I'm sweating like a pig. I can't even speak. I just push past him and go into the room. I'm terrified at what I'm going to see.

And what I see is my darling angel, asleep on the bed, with the TV on.

She never heard a thing.

And that is the very last time I will do anything like that again. Because look. I know you have to let them go a little bit.

Sometimes when we stay at a nice hotel we let them go to the pool by themselves, for example. I don't like it, but Laura says you have to give them a little bit of room.

But I don't like it. To this day, I don't like it. To this day, Ciara wants to go to a friend's house, I'm—what does she have to go there for? What's wrong with here? Here is good. Here is nice. Why can't she just stay here? You saw them all day at school. You want to see them? Go in your room, go to sleep, wake up, go to school, boom, there they are.

Ciara said to me this year: "Daa-aad, guess who's going to be seventeen next month," and I told her, "And you think you're gonna get to do anything you didn't do when you were sixteen? We had this conversation when you were fifteen and about to turn sixteen. I didn't say anything different then, and I'm not gonna say anything different now." She's waiting until she's eighteen, or twenty-one, because she thinks maybe things will change then.

All I can say is, if she's waiting for me to change, she'd better find a comfortable place to sit, because it's gonna take a while.

Not changing is one of the jobs that I do best.

There Is No "I" in Team, Except When I Choose the Teams

Another job that falls to the dad around this age is one of the most crucial ones that will determine your kid's personality for the rest of their lives. I'm talking, of course, about helping them make a very important decision.

Which team to root for.

That guy Bill Arnone I told you about, the one who did the "Judy Pazutti" games with his daughter—I met him when his girl and mine were pitching against each other in high school soft-ball. Great guy. Old-time Brooklyn Dodger fanatic—and I mean fanatic. He stayed with the Dodgers after they moved to Los Angeles and is a die-hard Dodger fan to this day. Well, one day, his daughter comes home and announces, I wanna be a Mets fan. All my friends are Mets fans.

The dad is brokenhearted. He doesn't know what to do. He begs, he pleads, he yells, he bribes, but there's nothing he can do but suck it up, buy her a Mets jersey, and take her to a Mets game at what was then Shea Stadium.

Not just any Mets game, though: a Dodgers-Mets game.

They go to the club restaurant, and who's sitting there but Tommy Lasorda, the longtime Dodger manager. Bill knows Tommy from a bunch of Dodger functions he's been to, so he goes over and introduces his daughter to Tommy. Lasorda takes one look at the Mets jersey and starts spewing out his spaghetti. "Oh, my God! You did this to your father? You became a Mets fan? How could you! Please! It's not too late! You're young! You can come back!" He's putting on a huge show. Everybody thinks it's really funny.

Except the daughter.

The next spring, the dad gets to throw out the first pitch at a Dodgers exhibition game at Vero Beach. His daughter is with him. While he's out there, who comes out to greet him but Tommy Lasorda himself.

The daughter takes one look at Tommy, turns, and runs like hell.

Was she scared straight?

Sad to say, no. Still a Mets fan.

Which only goes to show. You can set all the rules you want—but some things you just gotta accept.

Ain't easy.

But he got even when she went to college. She wound up in Boston. He agreed that she could go there, on one condition.

He gave her a bye on the Celtics—but he insisted that she may never, ever root for the Red Sox, Patriots, or the Bruins.

I mean, look. You gotta draw the line somewhere.

Repeat After Me: Time to Go, Time to Go, Time to Go

Most of the dads I know say there's another job that always falls to them. It's one they hate, and it's one they're really lousy at. I'm yet to find a dad who has any idea how to do this at all. But they all try.

That is, getting the family out of the house.

For this one guy, Jack, I know on Long Island, mustering the troops to get out the front door, like when you're trying to make a movie or something, was like one of those old-fashioned hand-held games where you have to get the five little metal balls into the five holes—just when you think you've got the last one, two of the ones you'd already gotten into the holes pop back out. In his case, he had four kids, ages four to fourteen, and it was always something—this one has to change her shoes. That one forgot to go to the bathroom. This one decides she can't leave the house without eyeliner. This one gets a cell phone call. This one just wanders off for no reason other than to drive Jack crazy.

But more often than not, it was the wife. Now granted, guys can get out of the house a lot easier than women can. Guy grabs a shirt off the floor, smells the armpits, decides it passes for clean, puts it on, buttons most of the buttons, looks in the mirror, sucks in his stomach, says, "Hey, lookin' good!" And he's ready to go.

Women, it's an endless loop: This blouse doesn't match that skirt. She changes the blouse. Now the necklace is too long. So she changes the necklace for a new one, which doesn't go with the earrings. New earrings, now the purse is wrong. New purse, bad shoes. Purse and shoes perfect, now she's gotta change the blouse. Repeat.

Here are the many brilliant things dads do through all this.

One: Stand by the front door and jingle the keys in your pocket. Dads believe this will somehow magically make the family members do what he wants them to do, which in this case is just please get to the car. It's just a movie. Batman will have gotten old and gray and traded in the Batmobile for a Hoveround by the time we get there. Let's go.

Two: Announce, in increasingly annoyed terms, what time it is. "It's five of, everybody! Let's go!" "Three minutes to seven! Come on!" "It's seven o'clock! Do you know where your children are?" This has as much effect on his family as reading pooper-scooper laws out loud has on your dog. No matter how much you do it, you still have to deal with the exact same amount of shit.

Three: Announce, in increasingly annoyed terms, how ridiculous this situation is. "Why does it take you guys so long to get out of the house?" "Do you know the movie is going to start?" "Am I talking to you or am I talking to the wall?"

(The answer, by the way, of course, is the wall.)

There are only three solutions to this.

One: Set every clock in the house ahead seven minutes.
Two: Set every clock in the house ahead nine minutes.
Three: Chill.

You can lie about how long it takes to get to wherever you're going, if you like; you can stomp and storm in the front hall like a caged cheetah waiting for feeding time; you can howl at the moon, also. Each of these will have about the same effect.

Big Daddy Trick: Sure, You Can Have a Phone

It seems like every time you turn around, you see younger and younger kids with their own cell phones. It's ridiculous, if you ask me. I swear, there's a seven-year-old on my block, kid has the latest iPhone. Talking to that Siri character all day, that voice in the cell phone that answers questions. What the fuck does a seven-year-old have to ask the cell phone? Kid: "Siri, where is the nearest candy store?" Siri: "You live next door to one. You asked me that yesterday. You ask me that every day. Please, someone, rescue me from this kid! I'll pay you money!"

But I will tell you this. As a Big Daddy, here's what you do: When your kids get a little older, when they ask for a cell phone, you make it the biggest deal in the world. You just keep acting like they're way, way too young. And then, at some point, you cave. Just give in. Trust me. The kid's gonna think she put one over on you.

Let her.

Because you just attached the greatest leash to the kid that was ever invented.

Now I gotta say, we never really had to worry about this with our girls. They were always really good about letting us know where they were. I don't know that they never lied to me, but I'd put good money on it, and I'm an old Vegas guy so I know how to figure the odds before I put a buck down.

But still, it kept me sane, having my girls have cell phones. I was always able to get a hold of them. You're going to a friend's house? Call me when you get there. Call me when you leave. Text me when you get out of the movies. To me, this is not a luxury. It's a necessity.

And that's with good kids. The weird thing is, now you have a

GPS in every cell phone, and the parents can actually hook it up to their computer and see where their kid is at any minute.

Would I have done that with my kids when they were younger? Maybe. Not because I think they were lying to me, but just in case of an emergency, you wanna know where they are.

I think on some level you gotta establish some trust with the kid. I would never, ever go through my kids' drawers, for example. I know a lot of parents who do that. I think it's pretty screwed up.

But knowing where your kids are? That's a no-brainer. It's just a good way to keep the dad calm.

Which in my case is not the easiest thing to do.

Who Do You Trust?

But this whole question of how much to trust your kids, that got tougher for me as the girls got older. Ciara, for example: Every time she leaves the house, she has to play Twenty Questions with me. And I'm not talking about, like, are you a public figure, living or dead. I'm talking about the real questions: Where are you going? When are you coming home? There's a football game? How are you getting there? Who else is going? Are you going to eat before or after the game? Where are you going to eat? Like I said, she hasn't lied to me yet, so I have no reason to believe she's lying. So I trust her. But I trust her because I know she hangs around the right kind of kids. And I know she hangs around with the right kind of kids because I make it my business to know who she hangs around with.

I always did. I mean, when they were younger, they went to school right next to the building where we were living. You didn't even have to cross the street to get to the school. From my door to the school was maybe like from home to first base. Maybe like a hundred feet. Didn't matter. They were going, I was going with them. Either me or my wife. Ciara was in the second grade, then. One of us was gonna walk her.

A little later, Bria was in junior high school. Eventually with Bria the school let the kids go out to lunch in the neighborhood. This is how crazy I was—I liked that they got to go out to lunch in the neighborhood. As long as they came to my apartment for lunch.

Six, seven, eight kids, they'd come up to the apartment. I'd come home at twelve o'clock and they'd all be there. Boys and girls. They'd bring their own lunches. I liked that they were comfortable to come hang at our apartment. That made me happy. It made me comfortable, too. I just don't like when they're out of my sight, unless I know they're in a safe place with a grown-up in charge. It just drives me nuts.

I don't know how parents can let their kids run around and not know what they're doing. Freedom to me is the worst thing to deal with. My wife is a lot better at this than me. She tells me, you have to let them go a little bit. I say, I don't mind letting them go, as long as one of us goes with them. She says, that's not letting them go. I say, why, they're going where they're going anyway, what's wrong with me being there?

That's when she shakes her head and leaves the room.

I get that a lot.

But these parents—I see packs of kids in the street late at night. Twelve, one o'clock in the morning. Girls who are thirteen, fourteen years old. What are you doing? Why are you out on the streets of New York City in the middle of the night? Who the fuck are these parents? They're teaching their kids freedom? They're teaching their kids to be independent? They're teaching their kids to be idiots, if you ask me. They're teaching their kids to do whatever the fuck they feel like doing, and get themselves into situations they can't handle. What, so as parents you can have some time to yourself? Then what the hell did you become a parent for? You want freedom, get a goddamn dog and hire the kid upstairs to walk it. But if you want to be a parent, then pay attention.

It was different when we lived in Las Vegas because they have to be driven everywhere. That helped a lot with my own particular kind of crazy. I hear parents bitch about having to be a goddamn cabdriver for their kids, I think, fuck that. Taxi driver? I'll put a goddamn meter in the car, hang one of those disgusting air fresheners from the rearview mirror, and talk on the cell phone in a foreign language all day if it means that I get to have my kids in the backseat with me driving them around. Kids are lousy tippers, though. There is that. But really—who complains about driving your kid around? Get over yourself.

I mean, I wasn't totally nuts. Pretty close, but not totally. When the girls were in junior high school, we let them have a little freedom—let them walk to go get a slice of pizza, go to the Shake Shack for a burger. But I wanna know where they're going, who they're going with, when they're coming home, and whether they're going to have cheese and onions on their hamburger. Well, maybe not the last thing, but you get my drift. You gotta picture the whole scenario, and you gotta walk them through it ahead of time. One, so you can have a little peace of mind. Two, so you can teach them to think ahead a little bit. Because that's the one thing teenagers are worst at, and the one thing Big Daddies are best at. So that's another rule you can live by. And that they can live by.

The Ugh Factor

In my house, I gotta say, we never went through the one thing my friends tell me is the hardest thing about having teenager girls.

For a lot of girls, there's this moment, around the time they turn thirteen, when they go into a dark tunnel and become the moodiest, grumpiest, meanest, most emotional creatures that walk the face of the earth. They emerge, when they're around twenty, and it's like nothing happened. But for a lot of my dad friends, it's a nightmare. My buddy Anson calls them the "ugh" years. When whatever you say to your daughter—clean your room, do your homework, act like a normal human being for five minutes—they turn, they roll their eyes, and they say, "Ugh." Anson used to say to his girls, "I know you're in there. When you're ready, come back out. Your room will be ready when you get back."

And it's not usually even the dad that gets the brunt of it all. It's the moms.

I'm not saying my girls and my wife didn't argue. Far from it—they argued all the time. Over big shit, over little shit. Over whether the girls could buy something, go somewhere, wear something, over whether they had to clean their room before or after dinner, whatever. But it never got into that I-hate-you stage that girls and their moms go into. I think I'm mostly just lucky. But I also like to think I had something to do with it—because there's no way I could stand for it. Like I've said, I'd let things get to a certain point, and then—bam! Out comes Big Daddy. You said WHAT to your mother? You said WHAT? It's like I'm just trying to get them to hear how they sound from somebody else's ears other than their own. I know, they're getting older, and they have to find a way to separate themselves from their mothers, I guess. And the hormones are raging like a fucking typhoon off the coast of Japan. It's calm one minute, and then the storm hits. Only the National Weather Service can't predict the storms that come out of a teenage girl when she's arguing with her mother.

Now, THAT would be an app for the iPhone you could make some money on. Anybody figures that one out, give me a call. We'll go halvsies.

But without that, the only thing I knew how to do was fight

fire with more fire. I'd let it go, and stay calm, for a couple of minutes. And then I wouldn't.

Worked for me, is all I can say.

Cool Papas

One of the calmest dads I know (in other words—one of the dads
least like me) is this guy Bob down in Virginia. Bob was a former
USA Today reporter, works for Homeland Security now. A real guy
job. But by night, he lives in The Land of Girls.

Bob was a divorced dad with custody of his two girls when he
met his second wife—who had three girls of her own. So when
they crammed into their little house in Virginia together, he found
himself living with five girls ages eight to fourteen.

If that doesn't take the patience of a saint, I don't know what
does.

It got pretty hairy, Bob said—girls can get pretty emotional
as they get to those "tween" years, and there was a lot of drama in
that house. But it was a lot of fun, too. "There was a lot of love and
dancing and laughter and jokes," Bob told me. "Nonstop. A lot of
positive energy."

Now, with my kids, I left a lot of the emotional stuff to my
wife, I'll admit. Because like I said, I was pretty lucky that my girls
didn't get into the I-hate-you-mom phase that a lot of girls get
into. From what I've heard from other guys, getting out of that
stuff happens about no times in a million. "You have to brace yourself for when they get into their teen years with their moms," Bob
said. "It's an emotional roller coaster. I've never seen it not be."

A lot of guys' strategy, when the going gets tough, is to put
their head down, head for their man cave, and come out when the
girls are about twenty. When they start screaming and yelling at
their moms, and the moms start screaming and yelling back, these

dads have another good strategy: Turn up the volume on the TV until you can't hear them.

But Bob took a different route, and you gotta give him credit, because what he says makes a lotta sense. "My goal was for them to have someone to talk to when things got weird," he said. "Because things do get weird."

So his deal—with his daughters and stepdaughters—was to hang back and make sure they knew they could talk to him about anything. "Girls are so sensitive. There's so much going on in their heads and their hearts. There's a lot of drama. It can be overwhelming. It can be confusing for them."

Amen to that. There's so much going on that can bust them apart when they're turning the corner to teenage-land. It's not enough to just make sure they're not screwing up at school, or being mean to the kid next door, or whatever. There's a lot they're gonna be going through. With boys, it's different—they wear the emotions on the inside. Maybe they're going through stuff, maybe not, but it's not all out there. With girls, it's out there. All the drama, all the time. They need to talk about it, and you gotta get your head in the game.

Especially in those years when everything's just too emotional with their moms. It's like being on the battlefield—sooner or later a bomb's gonna go off. Somewhere in there they're gonna need a calm, rational person to talk to—and you want it to be you, not some kid they met at school who's idea of good advice is to smoke a joint and forget about it all for a while.

So Bob says you gotta get in the game—even if that means letting them know they can talk to you about shit that you don't want to talk about.

It all came to a head for Bob one night when they had some friends over for dinner, and somebody told him that one of the girls needed him downstairs. She was in the bathroom, and he heard from through the door the one thing no dad ever wants to hear:

"I'm trying to put in a tampon and I can't get it in."

Calmly—like talking someone through disarming a bomb—he gave her instructions through the door. It worked. Nothing exploded, and he went back to the party.

First off, I'm glad that wasn't me. I don't know what the hell I would have said. But second—the fact that she was able to talk to her stepdad in a moment like that doesn't happen by chance. It happened because he'd spent years telling that kid that there's nothing she can't come to him with.

There's a Big Daddy for you.

My friend Hugh, the TV producer I told you about, says the emotional roller coaster is the hardest part for dads. Because what we're really, really good at is making it really, really worse.

"It drives me crazy," Hugh said. "Everything's great, everyone's happy, then all of a sudden some small thing makes one of the girls become unwound. And it's sort of like you put out the fire by negating what she's saying or saying, 'Hey it's not that bad, we can fix it,' but that seems to escalate it. It only makes it worse."

It's true, I think. A lot of dads walk around with what they think are fire extinguishers, but they're filled with gasoline.

"The good part is," Hugh said, "I've learned that it's an emotional roller coaster, but when they get out of control, they just as quickly calm down. Although, through nothing of your doing, of course."

The Confidence Game

But this all brings up another job that dads have to do as their kids grow older. This one's a little more serious. And it's one that dads are pretty lousy at.

Here's the thing. A lot of guys have this natural ability to act confident, usually without any good reason. But they walk around like the world is just sitting around waiting for the next brilliant thing to come out of their mouths. It starts early. On the playground, on the street corner, in the classroom. Guys just act confident like it's nothing. And the guys who don't have any confidence, they pretend that they do, so that the other guys don't stomp on them.

Of course, this is not true of every guy.

That's why some guys get stomped on.

But for the most part, that's what runs through the guys' side of the room: this overconfidence about everything. I can make that shot. I know that answer. I can take that guy. I can win this hand. (And later, unfortunately, I can have that one more drink and still drive home.)

That's the guys' side.

Girls are different.

With girls, there's an insecurity that starts early on. It hangs around them, like some annoying kid from down the block who won't take the hint and go home when dinnertime comes, and you wind up setting an extra place at the table, even though you know it's a mistake, and you don't want this kid hanging around with your kids. The habit of second-guessing themselves comes home with them like their fourth-grade homework, and settles in on the little pink chair next to the desk in their room and decides to stay for the next twenty years. For some, it never leaves. I have a friend whose wife ends every other sentence with, "Or maybe not," like she's afraid everything she says is wrong, and you listen to her and you think, I bet she's been doing that since the fifth grade.

So if you have a girl in the fifth grade, you gotta start listening for that.

And you gotta be the one to help her get over it.

Here's what I mean.

This woman I know, she's a big hotshot magazine editor. She has a simple explanation of how she got ahead: Whatever you do, do it with total and complete confidence. Whatever you say, say it with total and complete confidence. And when you're wrong, take the opposite position, and take it with total and complete confidence. This is the role model she set for her kids. That's the line she taught them.

The hotshot magazine editor has two daughters, and the younger one has some friends going to one of those "model U.N." things, where the kids pretend to be delegates to the United Nations and have to argue out some big issue. The night before the thing, two of the kids have to drop out, and she and a friend have to suddenly fill in. The girl is terrified. She doesn't know anything about the model U.N., anything about the issue, nothing. She's peeing her pants. And her mom, calm as day, tells her, "You're gonna do fine. Just say whatever you say with complete and total confidence."

And she did. And of course, the girl and her friend are awarded the "Best Delegate" award.

Now I gotta say, I think that mom is great. But—and I hope no moms are listening, but if they are, fuck it, I'm gonna say it anyway—guys are much better at this.

Or we could be, if we weren't such dicks.

Moms are usually not great giving their daughters confidence. One reason for this is that they grew up with the same insecurity.

The same treatment from the mean girls, the same self-doubts that their daughters are facing. Not all of them, of course. Just like not all guys are clueless, only most of us. But I'm just saying.

So when a daughter starts expressing that fear, that self-doubt, the mom is *not* the one who can put all the fear and doubt out of her own mind and say, "Fuggedabout it! You're gonna do great! You're the best!" The mom is not gonna say it and really, really sell it, anyway.

But this is where that stupid irrational overconfidence that guys have can really come in handy. If your daughter is starting to express that self-doubt—I can't try out for the school musical, I'm a lousy singer, say—you need to just lend some of that overconfidence to your daughter.

It's even more important than teaching her to throw.

Look, dads are judgmental. We just are. It comes with the territory. We can't help saying what our opinions are because they are, of course, brilliant. At least, when we do a survey of one person, which is ourselves, and ask ourselves if our opinion is brilliant, and the answer comes back yes, we figure, hey, 100 percent approval rating, I'm going to go with it.

And that's when we take the time to think before we speak, which is frankly not all too often.

So when your daughter wants to go to a movie with some friends and tells you who's driving, and we say, "That jerk is gonna drive? Over my dead body!," we know we are right because we have already checked with ourselves, gotten 100 percent support, and so we went with it.

Moms are the fountain of unconditional love. And that has its place. But when a mom says, "You're going to do fine, sweetie," it doesn't carry the same weight. Of course she's gonna say that. She's the mom.

But if you're a smart Big Daddy, and have let everybody know

you're a guy who will say whatever the fuck comes into his head—
"You know, if you don't wanna sing, you don't have to, maybe it's
better you just stay home"—when it's entirely possible that that
can come out of your mouth—then imagine the effect of that
overblown confidence when you say: "Of course you can sing!
You're the best singer I ever heard. No one sings like you! Who
can sing? Sally? She's a fucking squeaky gate! Pardon my French.
She's a goddamn squeaky gate is what I'm trying to say."

And even if your kid is a goddamn squeaky gate, she's going to
believe you.

And if you sold it right, she's gonna sing with confidence.
Complete and total confidence.

And you know what? I know a lot of singers. I know a lot of
singing teachers. And they all say the same thing: Confidence is
90 percent of what you need to be able to sing. The other 10 percent is also confidence.

What a coincidence.

Because life is just like that for a fifth-grade girl.

My kids, I'm lucky. They're pretty confident. Sometimes because they're good at stuff. And sometimes because they're brave.
But they're brave because their mother and I taught them early
on—or we tried to, anyway—that you don't walk into any situation
with your hand on the exit door. Whatever you do, you go in and
do it.

That magazine editor, I'll tell you, she deserves to be where
she is; not because she's the most brilliant editor in the world, but
because she can rally a roomful of big egos, get them all moving
in the same direction, get the best ideas out of them, weed out the
worst, and put on a damn good magazine.

And she never stops smiling. Like they used to say, woman's
got a smile so bright you know she shoulda been a candle. Smiling like she's on top of the world, even when the whole world is

crumbling down around her. When she feels confident she acts confident, and when she doesn't know what the hell she's talking about she acts confident about that, too.

I'm not saying you never criticize your daughter—exactly the opposite. The point of this whole book is, you gotta be critical and tough and mean and crazy and wild, when the situation calls for it.

But she's gotta know that she's still the star of your team. The franchise player. She's gotta know that no matter how crazy it may make you when she screws up, when she acts stupid or flunks a test or leaves a mess in the kitchen or forgets to call you when she's coming home late or the thousand other fucked-up things kids do to make you crazy, she's still the superstar, the absolute most fucking incredible kid you've ever known, and when she walks out that door, she's gotta act like it.

That's not so hard.

After all, *you* act like you're a superstar.

And look at what an asshole you are.

Nothing personal. I'm just saying.

The Bully on the Block

While we're talking about the difference between raising sons and raising daughters, I guess we oughta talk about the one scourge of both their lives, the one that comes in totally different forms for both of them.

I'm talking about bullies.

There's been a whole lot of talk about bullies in schools these days. And most of it centers around what schools should do. And that's all fine and dandy.

And not at all what we're talking about here.

What we're talking about is what parents gotta do.

And, more specifically, what dads gotta do.

But it's important to remember that it's different for boys and girls. They both get bullied just as much—but just in different ways from each other. You gotta know the difference, and you gotta give them the tools to get through it.

I know a guy named Willie who works at a clothing shop uptown. He has a son who's twelve and a daughter who's eleven, and they both just went through a session with a bully. And I think the way Willie dealt with it was pure Big Daddy material.

First, the son. The son, Anthony, comes home one day and says, "Dad, this kid Tyler has been hitting me on the bus."

First thing Willie does—Big Daddy point number one—is to say, "Okay, what did you do to bring it on? How did you piss this kid off?" Because you don't want your kid to immediately paint himself as the victim in every situation, which kids can do. "Hey, I'm not pulling the cat's tail, I'm just holding the cat's tail. The cat is doing all the pulling." "Dad! Billy hit my fist with his nose! Ow!"

Anthony assures his dad that it's not his fault. Turns out Anthony likes to sit next to the window, and so does Tyler, and when Anthony gets there first, Tyler tells him to move and whacks him a good one to make the point.

The next thing Willie does is ask the kid, do you want me to talk to the dad? Because sometimes getting hit by the bully isn't nearly as painful to a kid as having his dad go talk to the other guy's dad. I knew a lot of kids when I was growing up who'd rather take a beating than have their dad show up at somebody's house, so you gotta get that out of the way first.

But the kid says it's okay, so Willie goes over to talk to the dad, and figures this should be easy. The dad is a neighbor, and they've actually been pretty good friends—they've been over to each other's houses for dinner, the whole nine yards—so he thinks this won't take long. But he gets there, and guess what the dad says? He tells Willie that he thinks boys will be boys and that the dads shouldn't get involved, that the kids have to work this out for themselves.

Okay, let's get this straight right now. One of the main rules of being a Big Daddy is, you gotta sort out who the grown-ups are and who the kids are, and keep that straight. Kids don't learn to stop being assholes by magic. Kids learn to stop being assholes because you teach them the very complicated idea: Hey, stop being an asshole, kid!

So the fact that the dad won't step up pisses Willie off. "You know, I'm doing you a favor," he tells the dad. "Because one of these days your kid is gonna pick on the wrong kid, and he's gonna get his ass kicked."

"Well, then my kid will learn a lesson," the dad says.

So there's your point. You can either teach your kid the right values when you get the chance, or hope that at some point some thug will do the job for you. Great choice.

Willie gets it set in his mind that he's gonna take this to the teacher, to the principal, to the school board, whatever he has to do. But first, he's gonna do one thing that every Big Daddy has to do.

He's gonna teach his kid to stand up for himself.

He remembers a show on Animal Planet that they'd seen a couple of weeks ago. He tells Anthony, "You remember that show about the tiger chasing the gazelle? How the gazelle usually loses that fight, but this one time we saw the gazelle stop running and turn around and face the tiger, and the tiger was so confused, he just walked away?

"That," he said, "is what you have to do."

Anthony didn't like this idea. First, who the hell wants to be the gazelle? Second, what are the odds that the tiger's not gonna sink his claws into you anyway? But Willie is persistent.

"I don't want you to start anything," he says. "But if he hits you once, you hit him twice. He pushes you, you push him harder. He shoves you, you kick him as hard as you can. You might get beat up. But you're not going down without a fight."

Willie worries about this later. He wonders if he did the right thing. He worries that maybe he just got his kid to back the tiger into a corner, which is what you never want to do. He's seen enough Animal Planet to know that.

But a couple of days later, Anthony comes running off the school bus and up the steps. It was a Friday, and Willie was working the Saturday-to-Wednesday shift these days, so he happened to be home. "Dad! Dad!" he's yelling. The kid's bursting at the seams. Drops his book bag in the middle of the kitchen floor, and can't even sit down to tell his story.

Turns out Tyler came up behind Anthony on the schoolyard at recess that day. Did one of those things where he "accidentally" crashes his shoulder into Anthony as he walks by. Anthony spun around, slapped Tyler's arm with the back of his hand, and said, loud enough for everyone to hear: "Is that all you got? Come on, my little sister hits harder than that. Can't you do any better? Really? That's all you got?"

All the kids went silent. It was like that moment before the lightning hits, when everything's really still. They're all looking at Tyler, to see what he wants to do. Anthony's eyes are wide, and he's breathing heavy, and in that moment he feels like anything but a gazelle.

He has become a tiger.

Tyler doesn't know what to say. He turns and walks away.

"Just like that, Dad!" Anthony tells his dad. "Just like that! I did what you told me! I stood up for myself!"

Now look. I'm the first one to know that these stories don't always turn out like that. You remember that writer friend I was talking about, the one who told the stupid Schwartz jokes to his kid? He said he used to get beat up a lot when he was a kid. One time, he says, he got pissed off at this one bully who punched him in the nose for no good reason, and he just hauled off and belted the kid as hard as he could. Big roundhouse right to the temple.

That just made the bully angry, turns out. Writer friend got the biggest beating of his life. But you know what? He still remembers that punch. That one time he fought back. He remembers getting the shit beat out of him, of course, but more than that he remembers the feeling of saying, enough is enough.

And that's what you want your kid to learn. That sometimes you gotta say enough is enough. And that it might even be worth getting beat up for.

My writer friend says he usually got himself out of bad situations by making the bullies laugh. He says this one kid came up to him one time and started to threaten him, and he says to the kid, "Listen, you seem like a busy guy. How about I just beat the shit out of myself and save you the trouble? No charge. First one's free." Bully decides this is the funniest thing he ever heard, and not only doesn't he beat the writer guy up, they become friends, start hanging around together, and the bully starts protecting him. So, I guess there are other ways around the problem. But for me, those are small-odds bets. I guess, in a way, Willie's son used a little of both—a little standing-up-for-yourself, a little humor.

But the Big Daddy method is a lot more straightforward, and can be summed up pretty simply:

You mess with me, I'll mess with you.

So that's how Willie's son dealt with the bully, anyway.

Girl bullying is different. Girls don't hit each other as much. But they say the meanest, nastiest shit to each other. And for them, it's probably worse.

Willie's daughter, Nina, right around the same time, had this best friend, Rebecca, who was bullying another young girl, in the way that girls bully each other. She was saying, You can't sit with us at lunch, because we don't like you.

That's girl bullying. Willie gets wind of this, and gives it to his daughter straight.

What her friend Rebecca did to that other girl was mean and rotten, pure and simple. And you're a bully too, he said, because you didn't say anything to stop it.

Nina was pretty upset. She thought her dad was gonna take her side. She didn't want to sit with this other girl—she actually didn't like her much, to tell you the truth. And she sure didn't want to piss off her best friend.

You get to make the decision, her dad said. But I'm telling you which one is the right one.

A little while later, he heard Nina on the phone, telling Rebecca, What you did was wrong. It was mean, pure and simple. And it's not right for you to make me part of that.

Now, it's not often you hear your own words come out of your kid's mouth. But when you do, you know you did something right.

So here's what that Big Daddy did right. In both situations—with his son, and with his daughter—he helped them figure out how to navigate a tough situation. But that's not the main point. The main point is that in both situations, he jumped at the chance to teach his kids a core value. Look, there's gonna be times when what you gotta teach your kid is how to wimp out and run like hell, because that's the safest thing to do. There's gonna be times when what you gotta teach your kid is, don't get involved, it's not your fight, because that's the only way out. But those aren't the situations you gotta hunt for, and gotta be ready for.

You gotta hunt for situations where what you want your kid to do matches up with who you want your kid to be. You want your kid to be confident, and you want your kid to be kind. You want your kid not to be the one who does the easy thing; you want your kid to be the one who does the hard thing.

Confronting bullies, whether they're trying to stop some kid from sitting with you at lunch, or whether they're about to kick your ass, is one of those situations where your kid is gonna have to learn to do the hard thing.

And that's how you teach them how to be the kid you want them to be.

Is there a good chance the boys get a bloody nose off it, and will the girls get their feelings hurt off it? You bet.

Will they carry a little bit of their dad's values with them and—if you're really, really lucky—will they carry those values with them as they grow up, and maybe even pass them on to their own kids?

You bet.

Even Still More Great Moments in Big Daddy History

I was pretty lucky on this score. My kids go to a school where bullying is policed pretty close, and nobody gets away with much. Still, there are times.

A few years ago, some girl was picking on one of my kids pretty bad, on Facebook. Just saying some really nasty, ugly things.

Enter Big Daddy.

There are only two things that are good about being a little bit famous. Two things that I care about, anyway. One is that you get a good table at the restaurant. The other is when your kid needs help, you tend to have met some people who can help.

I call up this guy I knew, an ex-detective, and I tell him, my daughter's being tormented by some kid at school, via Facebook. Anything I can do about it? He tells me there's this whole cyber-bullying squad at NYPD, and he puts me in touch with them. I tell the squad, I wanna go down and confront the girl's father.

Who the hell lets his kid act like this? And if the dad doesn't know about it, why the hell not? He should know what's going on in his own house. So I'm ready to go down to this kid's house and tear the dad a new one.

I talked to the NYPD cyber-bullying guy and tell him I'm steamed as hell and ready to go get up in the face of the girl's dad. Guy at NYPD says, that's probably not a great idea. He tells me he's six-foot-four and 240 pounds, his partner is bigger than he is. Why don't you let us go down and say a pleasant hello to the dad and the daughter and see if we can't help them see the light a bit?

Sounded like a good plan to me. But after thinking it over, I called them back and said, no, I really wanna go have it out with this dad. NYPD guy says, tell you what. Why don't you try giving it a chance to just talk to the dad, calmly, on the phone, and feel out the situation. Give him the benefit of the doubt one time. So I give the dad a call, and I gotta say, he sounded about as flabbergasted as a guy could be. I mean, maybe he was acting, but maybe when he writes his daddy book it'll be called *You Never Know*. Because he swears he never knew. And he also swears that he'll take care of it right away.

And I gotta say, the problem stopped that very night. Suddenly all the ugly notes on Facebook were gone. Suddenly there's not a peep out of the other girl.

And suddenly, my daughter is actually hugging me and saying thank you.

So once again, my instinct of going down and tearing the dad a new one was wrong. Once again, cooler heads prevailed.

That's why you gotta sometimes take a minute and let someone else walk you through these things.

Because you never know.

There was another time I had to step in. This is a weird one. Some kid hits my daughter Bria, and word gets back to us. Laura tells Bria that she'll go talk to the kid's mom—only it turns out that the kid's mom is the teacher. We figure, okay, if anyone's gonna know how to handle the situation, it's a teacher. So I think it's all gonna be okay.

Think again. Laura talks to the teacher, and the teacher says she'll handle it, but the next day, her kid hits Bria again. Now Bria's coming home crying. I know she's a bit of a softie—Ciara's much tougher; Bria's gonna cry more easily—but still, if you make my kid cry, then you've crossed a line, and it's time to take care of the situation, fast. So my wife goes in there again, and what does the teacher say? "Well, we tried. There's not much we can do about it."

Not much we can do about it? What the hell kind of parent is this? There's a shitload of what we can do about it. You can punish your kid is what we can do about it. You can get in your kid's face and tell her exactly what's gonna happen if she hits Bria again, is what we can do about it. You can ground the kid for a few days or a few weeks or a few years for all the fuck I care, is what we can do about it.

But saying, "There's nothing much we can do about it," that's one of the things we absolutely cannot do.

So I said, Laura, you go back and you tell her, if this happens again, my husband is coming to see your husband. Don't threaten him, don't say, my husband is gonna beat up your husband. Just tell her I'm gonna come pay the man a visit.

Surprise. Kid never hit Bria again.

See, people can become real parents. You just gotta give them the motivation. If you told me my kid's hitting your kid, you can bet it'll be the last time. I don't understand this business, where parents think they aren't responsible. I don't know everything my kids do—I'm not with them all the time—but I assume if there's a problem I'm gonna hear about it, and you can assume that if I hear about it I'm gonna deal with it.

OPK (Other People's Kids), and Why They Drive Me Crazy

Now, in Vegas, I was involved in the kids' lives all the time. Part of that is just that when you live in the suburbs, like I've said, you've basically gotta drive them everywhere, and plan everything with the parents, and a lot of what goes on happens either at your house or at their house. When I was growing up, did my parents know my friends? They barely knew me, for all they saw me. I came home, dropped my books, changed my clothes, and out the door. But in Vegas, we knew all the kids' friends, pretty much.

And you wanna know something? For a guy writing a daddy book, I'm gonna be honest.

I don't really like kids that much.

I mean, I like *my* kids a lot. I like the way they act, I enjoy their company, they make me laugh, I make them laugh.

But it pretty much ends right there.

There are a couple of kids who I think are okay. Some kids downstairs, I've known them since they were babies, their parents adopted them from Taiwan, I like them. But they're pretty much the exception.

But I didn't stop them from coming around. We lived on a big lot in Vegas, an acre of land, and we'd throw these big parties for the kids on their birthdays. Because I was in the entertainment business, we had access to all sorts of things—one year we had a carnival with a pony ride and a Ferris wheel and carnival booths and all. And yeah, maybe we went a little overboard—but nothing, I mean nothing, compared to what I saw a little ways down the road. These friends of my kids had sweet sixteen parties that cost more than a Porsche! (And they'd get a Porsche on top of it.) It was insanity. When Bria turned sixteen, Laura said she wanted to take her and a bunch of friends down to Florida. When I heard what the airfare was gonna be, I went through the roof. They could have flown to Florida on Air Steve, I was so over-the-top furious. I got lucky, though, because when you're in my business you have connections to people who can get things done. This guy I know says, "I have a plane. You can use my plane." So we actually flew the kids down to Florida on a private plane, and flew them back. The sweet sixteen of a lifetime, if you ask me.

But anyway, when they were little, we'd have these big parties, maybe twenty or thirty kids. The shindigs didn't cost me much; I mostly had guys I would book in the clubs, and pay them a few extra bucks to do my kids' parties. Magicians, or a guy who released a dozen white doves, that sort of thing. At Christmas, we had a Santa Claus come, and I'd put a little earphone in his ear, and I'd have a mike hidden away, and Laura would whisper little personal things about the kids in his ear.

That was nice. I liked that.

The kids, I didn't like as much.

This bunch of kids would be screaming and yelling and bouncing around like lunatics. It made me crazy. We had a guy dressed up as Elmo, and this one kid is pulling Elmo's tail like he's trying to yank it off—and the parents are watching and they don't say a fucking word!

And what gets me even more is the parents who just drop the kids off, like you're the babysitter. So now you're trying to control a room full of monkeys, and you're the only trainer in sight. It was obnoxious. Because they were obnoxious.

I know my kids didn't behave at other people's houses like that, because either I stayed, or Laura stayed. Which, if it was me, was difficult, because, if I haven't mentioned it, I really don't like kids.

I don't like a lot of parents either, to be honest. That's the other thing about your kids' friends at school. Now you gotta hang around with their parents, just because they happen to have given birth to someone that your daughter likes to hang around with,

which is not my idea of a good reason to be friends with somebody. Maybe somebody likes to play poker, knock back a beer, tell
raunchy stories—these are good starting points. We both have a
kid the same age—that's like some random dating service for parents who don't actually want to meet anyone. But there you are. So
you talk and try to be nice, but the dad's an asshole. Or the dad's
okay and the mom's a nutcase.

And for this I'm giving up my Saturday afternoon.

If that's not a guy who loves his kids, I don't know what is.

8

THE BOYS ARE BACK IN TOWN

There comes a point in every dad's life when his daughter is gonna start dating.

Around age forty is good, if you ask me.

Problem is, they didn't ask me. I don't care who you are, when your daughter gets to the point where there are boys around, either you think it's horrible beyond belief, or you're lying to yourself. There is no third option.

I ran around a lot when I was a teenager, and I can't help it—I see a boy within ten feet of my beautiful daughters, and I remember when I was a teenage boy, and it's all I can do not to slap him silly just for what I think he's thinking.

When it comes to talking about my daughters, I'm not even comfortable thinking about what you think that kid is thinking about.

There was one friend of ours, I heard her at a party, talking about her daughter, and she said, "Yes, my daughter is very popular. She has many, many, many boyfriends," and I'm thinking, she's seventeen. This cannot be a good thing. You don't brag about something like that. Lot of boyfriends? You don't say that with pride. You start looking up a good nunnery.

I've had friends of mine who have handled it different ways. I have one friend who says to me, "My daughter and I are very close. She tells me everything. I know who she's dating, what they're doing, everything." I'm thinking, Good for you. You know what? I don't want to hear everything. I don't want to hear ANYTHING. You kissed a boy last night at the dance? Good for you. Go tell your mother. Or tell me where he lives and he won't have any teeth anymore. That guy who let his daughters know they could talk to him about everything? God bless him. Better man than I am. I'll send my daughters over to your house. They can talk to you.

There's nothing wrong with this. I've had it up to here with the idea that dads have to be as sensitive as moms. Dads have a lot of jobs. Big Daddies have even more. Hearing them talk about kissing boys doesn't have to be one of them. Listen, they're my babies. I understand they're growing up, and the rest of the world can treat them as little adults, and their mom can be as reasonable as she wants. I say, there's a need for one unreasonable parent in the house. And I'm happy to fulfill the role.

Why? Because kids are going to rebel anyway. If you set the bar too low, they've gotta go really far to rebel. And you don't want them to go that far.

Case in point: my friend Pauly. His wife had a kid from a previous marriage, and she was really lenient with the girl, and Pauly knew enough not to stick his nose in too far. But when he did get involved, he plotted the strategy like a chess master.

The girl, who was twelve, wanted to get her ears pierced. The mom didn't think this was a big deal. Pauly said, make it the biggest deal in the world. Tell her you'll think about it. Act like you're struggling over the decision. Finally give in and tell her she can get her earlobes pierced—but ONLY her earlobes—when she is thirteen. So the thirteenth birthday comes around, she gets the ears pierced, and right away she wants more piercings. The top of the ear, the nose, the whole bit. Same plan: Make a huge deal. Say absolutely not for a while, then finally give in. Tell her, okay, you're caving. Top of one ear when you're fourteen. Top of the other ear when you're fifteen. Dye your hair green? seventeen.

The girl's twenty-one now. Pauly's take on the situation? "Hey, she's the only one of her friends who managed to make it to twenty-one without a tattoo. By me, that's victory."

And that's my point. You're not there to be friends with your daughters. You're there to be their dad. You're allowed to make a big fucking deal out of little things. That way, when they get to the big things, they'll recognize them sooner.

At least, that's the theory. Doesn't always work in practice. But so far, so good.

Joe Medeiros, my buddy from *The Tonight Show*, had a different take on the hair thing. I think this one was brilliant. His son wanted to dye his hair fire-engine red one summer. Joe said, "Okay, but on one condition—you don't dye it back. You want it, you keep it." Kid says, "Okay, you got a deal."

Well, first couple of weeks, the kid is thrilled. Joe just bides his time. Because after a couple of weeks, from the chlorine in the pool or whatever, it turns a kind of ugly orange. Then, as it grows out, it's kind of ugly orange with brown patches. Kid never said a word about it, but once it grew out long enough to cut it, he never asked to dye his hair again. Sometimes, you gotta let them figure things out for themselves—but sometimes, you can kinda set up the lesson so they manage to trip over it and not know you put it there.

Joe had another really good strategy for dealing with his kids. Joe, you should know, was one of the guys who created the "Jay Walking" segment on *The Tonight Show*. In fact, he's the one who came up with the name. If you never saw it, it's one of the funniest, and one of the scariest, bits they ever did. Funny, because Jay Leno would walk up to people and ask something simple, like, "What country did we fight in the Revolutionary War?" and they'd say, "Vietnam." Or "Name a country that borders the United States," and they'd say, "Europe." And that last one was a college kid!

"We were constantly seeing what people don't know," Joe said. "Kids can name all the Kardashians, but they don't know what year they fought the War of 1812."

So when his daughter announced she wanted a phone in her room—yes, this is before cell phones, that's how old we are—he figured this was a chance to get her to at least learn a few things. He told her if she could memorize the fifty state capitals, he'd get her the phone. "I assumed she'd never do it," Joe admitted. "I figured I'd never hear about it again." But a week later, she came back and said, "Okay, I'm ready. Test me." And sure enough, she knew the capitals. And she got the phone.

So, maybe she actually learned something that week. So, maybe Joe did, too.

I Think Ink Stinks

But the tattoo thing, that's the biggest fear you have. Well, not the biggest. But pretty big. I know there are parents that allow it. Like the mom I told you about who went off to get a mother-daughter tattoo with her kid, like it's some brilliant bonding thing. I read about this one guy in New York, a tattoo artist, who tells the moms and daughters, "Get the fuck out of here. I will not tattoo a mother and a daughter."

I wanna give that guy a medal.

I just told my kids, flat out, no tattoos. No bargaining, no discussing. Just no.

When you're older, you wanna get a little tattoo where no one can see it, I still think it's idiotic, but okay, that's your decision. But until you're twenty-one, you think I'm gonna let you make a decision that affects you for the rest of your life? No way.

My girls had their ears pierced when they were babies. I let one of them get a second piercing after she graduated high school. And then the other day I saw she did another one. And I went ballistic. You did what? What is that? You know, she's twenty, but I still gave it to her. What are you doing? This does not make me happy. This does not make me happy at all.

She didn't say anything, and I know I was pretty rough on her, and I know it upset her. But guess what. That, my friends, is another rule I live by. I don't wanna upset my kids. But that's never, ever gonna be my first priority. My first priorities are gonna be keeping them safe, teaching them values, making sure they are growing up to be good people, keeping their heads outta their asses. And if I gotta upset them once in a while to make my point, I can live with that.

And you know what? So can they. This didn't do permanent damage to our relationship. (To be honest, it didn't even do permanent damage to her ear.) But she heard me.

And she heard me well enough that I don't think she'll come home with a tattoo.

These kids, I see them with all these tattoos—they're so limiting. You wanna be a barista at Starbucks with the fucking Sistine Chapel tattooed on your arm, good for you. But who the hell is gonna hire you for a real job? What are you gonna do when you're thirty, wear long-sleeved shirts all your life? It's insane. You wanna get a tattoo? Get the words "no tattoos," and tattoo it on the bathroom mirror. That'll do for now.

The Big Daddy of All Big Daddies

See, this whole protective thing, this whole Italian thing, it goes way back. I told you for me that I think it started when the girls were born. But actually it's more ingrained than that. It goes all the way back to when we were kids.

My buddy Jimmy has the best story about this. His mom, Emily, and her brother, John, got put in a home when they were young. It was the Depression, and their dad had died. Their mother had to work a double shift in the coat factory, so she couldn't take care of the two kids.

So John decides he's gonna watch out for his little sister. Always protective of her, always keeping an eye out for her. This goes on, and now John is seventeen, and Emily is fifteen, and this guy comes around, wanting to date Emily.

But to get to date Emily, the guy has to go through John.

"You wanna date my little sister, you talk to me," John says. Mind you, the guy is three years older than John—but John's a tough little bastard. He tells the guy, "You can go out with her, but I bring her to the date, and I bring her home."

So there is the guy at the movie theater, and John and his sister come down the street, on a bicycle. He doesn't even have a car. She's on the handlebars, and John is driving her. They come up to the guy, and John says to him, "Buy me a ticket so I can sit behind you guys."

The date ends, and John puts his sister on the bike and off they go. "You want to take my sister out again," John says, "you talk to me."

The guy, of course, turns out to be Jimmy's dad. Fortunately, he persisted in trying to date Emily, or Jimmy wouldn't be here today.

But John, that tough little bastard, never changed his ways.

When John got married, he had a couple of sons and a daughter. Jimmy and his brothers would go over to visit Uncle John, and all the cousins would play together, but it was really clear that the rules were different for the boys than for the daughter, Mary.

"This poor girl, can you imagine growing up as the daughter of this guy?" Jimmy said. "We go to this house, we have to sit on furniture with plastic on it, he's got velvet ropes on rooms that people aren't allowed to go in, it's that kind of house.

"The adults could go up in the kitchen, and the kids were in the basement or in the yard. And it was, 'Mary—sit with your legs closed!' All the time. She's on the swings—'Mary! Close your legs!' 'But Dad, I'm on the swings.' 'Close your legs or get off the swings! Go sit over there!' The boys are playing. She wants to play. She can't. Because she's a girl, she has to sit like a lady, with her legs closed and her hands folded on her knees, like a confirmation picture. She has to live her life looking like a confirmation picture."

Mary turns out fine—grows up, gets married, becomes a brilliant doctor. And Jimmy says, "While you couldn't raise a girl today the way Mary was raised, there's something to be learned from Uncle John."

It's this: The family is a protected unit, and the father is the padrone, the protector.

Today, Jimmy's dating a woman with two daughters who are sixteen and fourteen. And even though they're not his own girls, he's still the male presence in the house, and he looks the boys over when they come to call.

"There's a way guys can communicate with each other, even if one is sixteen and the other is fifty. They can look at each other, and you know you better behave, without saying a word. A guy walks into a house where there's no male presence. He feels a little more empowered, I think. There's got to be some fear. Because fear leads to respect."

And I think there's a lot of truth in what Jimmy's saying. He never thought his uncle was strange—we didn't form opinions of older people like that. We just figured, they're the ones in charge, and so we did what they said. Kids have a lot of other ways of knowing about the world these days—a billion other ways—so they're quicker to say, "No, you're wrong, Dad. That's not the way it is."

Which is why you gotta be more forceful, sometimes, and say, No, YOU'RE wrong. My way is the way it is, and as long as you're in my house, my way is the way it's gonna be.

And P.S., while you're at it, close your legs.

Mistakes Worth Making

There's an invisible switch that flips in every kid's head at some point, at which time they start wanting to be anywhere their parents are not. They just start showing this independent streak and wanna start doing lots of stuff on their own.

I'd like to figure out how to flip the circuit breaker on that switch, or a least put a dimmer on it. But unfortunately kids' wiring is a little tougher to figure out than the electricity in a condo.

And the monthly fees are a lot higher, too, but that's another story.

I think it's a fine line, when your kids turn that corner, between keeping a careful eye on them—or a big fat thumb on them, if you wanna know what I really think—and acting like you don't trust them.

I mean, you don't trust them. But you can't act like that.

Let's face it, any parent who could, would have one of those Google Street View cars following their daughters around, and would stay glued to the computer screen all day, watching their every move and taking screen grabs for later conversation. ("Right here—corner of Twenty-Seventh and Fifth, 1:37 p.m. Who is that boy? And where, exactly, is his hand?")

But you can't do that. One, Google doesn't rent out the cars. But two, like I was saying earlier, you can't treat your kids like you just don't trust them. I knew this one guy, used to ask his daughter where she was going. This was when she was just starting high school. He'd ask her and then suddenly show up there unannounced a little while later.

That's cold. I've never done that, and I would never do that. You gotta trust your kids until they give you a reason not to, and then you gotta get them in the habit of trying to win your trust back. But they have to know that it's possible, or they won't try. Kids really want you to trust them, and they'll actually work at earning that trust if you give them the chance to. If they know they have no chance, they won't make the effort.

And I think I've made it clear by now that I'm not above embarrassing my kids in public when there's a reason to—but there's got to be a reason to. Showing up is embarrassing, and you can't just show up for no reason. I've had things where my daughter said, "What, you don't trust me?" and I've said, "You, I trust. It's other people I don't trust." So if she's going somewhere where I know there's gonna be liquor, for example, I might make an appearance. But I'll let her know I'm coming, and I'll let her know when I'm gone.

And then I'll sneak around the corner and watch with a little pocket mirror. But don't tell her that. I don't want her to think I don't trust her.

But there's a serious point to letting your kids know you trust them. And it has to do with teaching them to be independent, because for them to learn that, then you're gonna have to let them make mistakes every once in a while.

There's a whole lot of talk these days about "helicopter parents." Parents who hover, who are there for their kids every minute. Who are in the kid's face every time she gets an A-, who are on the teacher's case every time the kid gets a B+. I've been talking a whole lot about how important it is for dads to get in there and be involved with their kids, but it's important to remember that you can carry that too far.

So you gotta let kids make mistakes sometimes. Within reason, of course. You don't let them juggle knives or date the local heroin dealer. But if they don't fall down once in a while, they're never gonna learn to pick themselves up. That's the only way they're gonna learn to take responsibility for their own lives. And that's a skill that Big Daddys have to teach their kids.

Here's an example. Every parent who has had the kids beg for a dog has heard the same line: "Daddy, I promise, I'll walk the dog, I'll feed it, I'll clean up after it." And so you get the dog, because you think it'll teach the kid some responsibility. And after the first month, the kid gets bored of walking the dog in the rain.

And so the parent starts walking the dog, and saying, oh, you kids, you know you're supposed to be doing this, and the kids are saying, oh, Dad, be quiet. We're trying to watch *The Twilight Saga*.

So tell me. Who exactly is in charge of *this* family?

But it's not just a matter of the kids taking over your world, which is bad enough. It's a matter of the kids learning to take over their own world.

And there's only one solution to it.

You gotta, at some point, let that dog take a shit on the kitchen floor.

My buddy Joey actually did this. He was having to nag his kid, every day, walk the dog, walk the dog, walk the dog. The kid moaned and complained like he was being put on KP and it was onion day at the camp. But Joey held fast: You said if I got the dog, you would walk it. So walk it.

This went on for a couple of weeks. Finally, Joey decided on a different plan. He stopped harping on his kid about walking the dog. He stopped reminding him. He stopped everything. He told the kid, If you don't feed the dog, he doesn't get fed; if you don't walk him, he doesn't get walked. Joey make a little chart that they hung on the refrigerator, so the kid could keep track of walking the dog three times a day, and feeding it twice, and filling the water bowl.

It was like setting a mouse trap. Joey knew it would only take a couple of days for it to spring.

Sure enough, about three days later, his kid forgot to walk the dog at night. The next morning, the kid walked into the kitchen and stepped right in a big warm pile of dog shit.

There is nothing, and I mean nothing, that will teach a kid a lesson faster than that. Did the kid wail to the high heavens? You bet.

Did the kid remember to walk the dog after that?

You bet.

But don't take this too far. The whole idea of letting them make their own mistakes—that's fine up to a point.

But only up to a point.

When kids start making big mistakes—this one wants to drop out of college, that one wants to quit her job—a lot of parents say, Well, that's their life to live. They'll learn from their mistakes.

The hell they will.

When it comes to real-life decisions, I don't buy the idea that you learn from your mistakes. I think, go ahead and learn from other people's mistakes. This guy didn't study for a test and flunked out of school, that guy got drunk and wrapped his car around a telephone pole, this girl didn't use protection and now she's knocked up at seventeen years old and her life is fucked. What, you gotta let your kid go through all that to learn from her mistakes? Look, there's plenty of mistakes all around you. Watch those. Learn from those. Your kid has got exactly one life. You're gonna let her waste half of it screwing up so she can learn from that and maybe salvage the other half? What the fuck kind of logic is that?

My kids don't have to learn from their mistakes. Hell, I've made enough mistakes in my life. They can learn from mine.

It's Midnight—Do You Know Where Your Kids Are?

For me, if there's one rule that everybody's gotta know as their daughters start going out at night—and start staying out later, and wanting to stay out later—it's this:

Nothing good happens after midnight.

That's it. That's the bottom line. There was this song, when I was growing up that went, "After midnight, we're gonna let it all hang out." Well, you know what? That's as good a reason as any for my kids to be home at 11:59. I don't even wanna think about what letting it all hang out means today.

Look. I know kids are gonna do what kids are gonna do. That's my point. I don't need my kids to be hanging around with them while they're doing it. We read in the paper about these two girls, from uptown. Pretty girls. Young, in their twenties. They weren't junkies—but they were fucking around with heroin. Recreational, you know? They're down on the Lower East Side, bought some heroin, snorted it. Both of them died.

I mean, I know this is supposed to be a funny book, and I'm not trying to get too heavy here, but at some point you have to face the fact that when you look at the kids around your kids, some of them are going to make some bad choices.

This one guy I know, his daughter was twenty-two. She told him, out of the blue, that she was thinking of taking LSD. Now,

I would have just locked my daughter in her room until she was old enough for social security, but this guy decided on a different approach. He was this old hippie guy who had done acid himself back in the day, and he'd been honest and told his daughter that. So instead of just telling her "no," he decides to just let her know how very, very scary it can be. How if you're gonna do it, make sure you do it with somebody you trust, somebody who's done it a lot, somebody who's talked a lot of people down from bad acid trips.

"You mean, like you?" she asked.

"Well, that's one possibility," he said.

Somehow, that took the wind out of her sails. Doing acid with your father, I guess, is way down the list near getting drunk with an insurance salesman. She never did it.

But you do whatever you gotta do—like I said, that wouldn't have been my approach, but whatever works, works.

The question of how late they can stay out goes back to the whole Vegas idea. You can't ever really beat the house, but if you play smart you can increase your percentages. Don't throw five bucks on four the hard way, don't hit when the dealer's showing a six, and don't let your kids stay out after midnight.

I don't want my kids taking the train at twelve o'clock at night. Me, I used to take the train to Brooklyn when I was eighteen—I was a college freshman, going to John Jay. A bus to the train, a train to the junior varsity game. Sometimes I was coming home at two, three in the morning. I mean, I was a big, tough, strong guy, and I still think I was really lucky to have survived that. I'm gonna put my sixteen-year-old daughter on that train?

I don't think so.

I want them to take a cab if they're coming home after dark, but then I read about a cab driver who raped this girl, so now I gotta worry about that?

It makes me crazy. And there's no reason for it.

So you gotta draw the line someplace. And a good place to draw the line is where the fairy godmother drew it. Midnight comes, everybody turns back into pumpkins and mice, so get yourself home before that.

If Cinderella can make it home, you can, too.

9

ON THE BALL

talked before about what happens when girls get involved in sports when they're little. But high school sports are a whole different story. Ever since Title IX, girls' sports have become a big deal. And God bless: All those girls who are going to college on lacrosse scholarships or tennis scholarships, all I can say is it's about time.

But for a dad, whose high school daughters happen to be good enough to make the team, it can be torture.

Trust me. I know.

For one thing, the whole question of how much is too much—when are you being the Big Daddy who's there for his kid, and when are you being the overprotective asshole who can't keep his big mouth shut—that gets all out of whack when it comes to sports.

There's a fine line between cheering for your kid and screaming like a maniac. Unfortunately, it only seems like a fine line because so many parents crossed it so far back, they can barely see it anymore. I've been to dozens of softball games that Ciara has played in, and the way some dads behave, I just want to slap them.

A couple of times I almost did. The fact that I didn't is a testament, I think, to my restraint and good judgment, and also to the very strict laws in New York State regarding assault.

When it comes to sports, I just wanted my girls to get a fair shake. I know how to get along. I'm not a shy guy, but I'm not a raging lunatic. I just see how people throw their weight around.

They start early. Badgering the coach, annoying the assistant coach, making a couple of veiled threats to the head of the athletic department. And it's worse in private schools, because these are well-off folks who are already in the habit of throwing their weight around, so it comes naturally. But public or private school, doesn't matter, you show me a kid who's not pitching as many innings as her mom thinks she should, and I'll show you the potential for a big-pain-in-the-ass mom having conversations with the coach she shouldn't be having.

And sometimes it's the coach's fault, because he's worse. I got this one buddy, his kid pitches Little League and had a couple of bad outings. Coach is real nice about it, tells the kid, just because you had a couple bad outings doesn't mean you're off the mound. I need you out there. You're gonna get out there again.

And then the kid never gets out there again. Coach pitches his own kid, and the assistant coach's kid, every game. Doesn't matter how bad their kids screw up—and a couple of times they screwed up pretty bad—their kids keep going out there. My buddy's kid never pitches another inning. He decides he doesn't want to be one of those interfering parents, so he doesn't say anything.

Too bad I wasn't there. Because if it was my kid, I woulda said plenty.

My point is, I know all this politics is going on. I'm not gonna be like that crazy mom who yells at the coach until he puts her daughter in. But I'm not gonna ignore the situation. I'm gonna watch my kid's back, and if she's getting the short end of the stick because some full-of-himself dad is pushing the coach to bench my kid for his, or some idiot coach can't see past his own kids' needs to give a fair shot to the rest of the team, I'm gonna open a mouth, and believe me, I got a mouth to open.

Fortunately, so far, it hasn't come to that.

I mentioned before that I was pretty good at sports myself when I was a kid. You wouldn't know it to look at me now, but I had the athletic build, and the reflexes to go with it. There was a time in my life that there was nothing I would rather do, I mean nothing, than play basketball. I played for Brooklyn College, and in the summer I was a counselor at camps in Monticello, in what New Yorkers call "upstate" and what everybody else in the state calls "just outside the city." Then later, when I was working, I played five nights a week, in leagues all over the city, from Bed Stuy to Sunset Park to Bensonhurst to Staten Island, and on and on. I was fanatical. Passionate as passionate can be. In the end, I guess I had more passion than talent, but I made the most of what I had. And I understood how much of your sense of who you are can get caught up in how you play.

Ciara's been playing softball since she's five, and she loves to play. Like I said earlier, it's different with boys and with girls. Boys like to play ball, but it's expected of them, too. With girls, if they don't want to play, nobody looks at them sideways. And if they play really well, like Ciara does, there's something extra special about it, just because it's unexpected.

We certainly didn't force it on her. Our philosophy was, when the kids were growing up, let's introduce them to everything. Bria took guitar lessons, Ciara took keyboard. They took gymnastics, they took dance. Bria was good at gymnastics; Ciara was good at art. That's how we wanted it to be—give them a chance to find their own thing, and see what they latch on to. They're not gonna latch on to everything. I don't agree with the Tiger Mom idea of forcing the kid to play the violin or whatever, and making them practice whether they like the damn thing or not. I mean, they gotta do something—they're not gonna sit in their room with the shades down and play video games—but they get to find what it is they're passionate about.

I could tell early on with Ciara that softball was gonna be a passion for her. I could also tell early on that I was gonna have to bite my tongue a lot around the other dads. I mean really—ten years old, Little League, and you're gonna be yelling at the umpire, challenging a call for half an hour? You're gonna ridicule the members of the other team? Who does this?

Nut jobs, is who does this. And there's a lot of nut jobs out there. I'm telling you, when it comes to sports, you gotta be the Big Daddy times ten—you gotta push your kid to succeed, and you gotta know when to back off. You gotta have their back when somebody screws with them, but you gotta keep your yap shut 90 percent of the time.

I did push my kids—but I pushed them to try hard. To give it their best. Same as when Bria was playing basketball when she was younger, and I told her you're not gonna get better by magic over the summer, you gotta practice every day. Same with Ciara and softball. I just wanted to see her out there, taking her swings, going to the batting cage, practicing her pitching. Getting her butt out and her glove down on a grounder. Having a humble attitude when you win and a good attitude when you lose. I didn't care if she got to be great at the sport. I really didn't. I wanted her to, for her sake, of course. But it was more important to me that she keep it in perspective.

And that I keep it in perspective.

Which is when I started with the headphones.

It got to the point where I couldn't keep my mouth shut anymore. These parents, screaming at their kids after every play. Screaming at the other team. Screaming at the umpires. Yelling

like they're at Yankee Stadium in the third row in the fourth inning after the fifth beer.

So I took to sitting in the outfield, down the left-field line,
and watching the game with headphones on. I'd listen to Sting,
or Dave Matthews, or Van Morrison, or whatever, and watch the
game and keep my mouth shut.

At least part of it, I have to be honest, was also to keep the
parents from yakking at me. As annoying as the yellers were, the
yakkers were almost as bad. You're here to watch your kid play ball.
Why don't you watch your kid play ball? This isn't the time to tell
me what your favorite Italian restaurant is in the Village, or what
you think of Obamacare, or how great your summer place in the
Hamptons is, you self-centered fuck. Shut up and watch the game.
Do I come to your house when you're doing whatever the hell it is
you like to do, and tell you about my place in the Hamptons? No,
because I don't know where you live, I don't have a place in the
Hamptons, and, most important, who gives a fuck.

And part of it, also, was to try to keep myself calm, because
when Ciara's on the mound, I get as nervous as hell.

It was almost as bad with Bria before her. I remember the time
Bria played in an All-Star softball game up in Harlem. She's in
the seventh grade, and some of these girls are in the tenth grade,
they're twice her size, and I'm shitting my pants because I'm
thinking, Bria's team is not that good, and they're gonna get killed.
Well, she comes up to bat, bases loaded, and I was ready to faint,
I'm so nervous. Pitcher windmills one in, and the sound of that bat
slamming the ball is still echoing somewhere in my head. Smacks
a line drive up the middle, and it's one of the greatest moments.

But Bria is more of a girlie girl; she wasn't as competitive as
Ciara, not into it as much. So when Ciara's on the mound, I know
her whole heart and a good chunk of her self-esteem are out there
with her. And so I'm nervous as hell.

She had to sit out most of her freshman year because of a

stress fracture in her back that she got from pitching. But last year, as a sophomore, she was already pitching for the varsity at her school in Brooklyn. And I gotta say, that takes some balls, to be sixteen years old and standing on the mound with a big crowd watching your every pitch.

Now, you gotta wonder how much it's worth it for kids in this situation. For every winner there's a loser. Is it worth it to put your kid through this pressure, knowing that if she fails, it's gonna weigh on her for a long time, maybe she's gonna carry that with her for the rest of her life—I mean, it's just a ball game, but for a kid, it's everything.

I say yes, it's worth it. Win or lose. Fly or fail. Because if they win, they'll walk away with a confidence that they also get to carry with them. And if they lose, they learn a lesson about picking themselves back up—or at least, they have the chance of learning that lesson. If their Big Daddy helps them to.

We're uptown for a big game. Huge crowd. The starting pitcher for our team gets into trouble and we get behind early. They bring in Ciara, she calms everything down and proceeds to pitch a terrific game. In the meantime we rally to tie the score.

So now it's the bottom of the last inning. Score is still tied, but they get two on. It's second and third with two outs, but the batter coming up is a girl that Ciara's gotten out twice before.

And then the coach does about the dumbest thing he could do. He tells Ciara to walk the batter. Walk the bases loaded with two outs! Craziest thing I ever heard. Maybe in the majors you do that, and then only if there's one out, to set up a double play and maybe get out of the inning. But for a teenage girl, to put that kind of pressure on her? It's like he's trying to jinx my daughter. I saw the look on her face—she coulda been three years old again out there. She's so confused. But she does what the coach says and walks the batter. So now it's bases loaded. I'm thinking, fuck, now anything bad happens, and it's game over.

And sure enough, the next batter comes up, and Ciara bears down, and her arm windmills around, and I don't see anything wrong, but the moment she releases it I can tell she's freaking out, and it all happens in slow motion for me: The ball hits the batter. The ump signals for her to take her base. The runners all advance. The girl on third comes home.

And we lose the championship game.

Ciara, who normally is really great at keeping it together, bursts into tears. "I'm sorry, Daddy," she's crying to me. "He told me to walk her! He told me to walk her!"

I wanted to put the coach up against the wall. I started moving in the direction of the coach, and it was pretty clear what my intent was.

And then I felt a hand on my arm.

"Don't do it, Daddy," Ciara said through her tears. "Don't say anything."

I looked over at the coach. I wanted to tell him to apologize, and if he got shitty with me, I was gonna slap him until I made him cry like he made my daughter cry. And I'm not ashamed for one second to admit that.

But then I looked at my daughter. And in that moment, I realized: I have to let her do this her way. Not mine. If she wants to handle it, I have to let her handle it.

Sometimes being the Big Daddy means stepping in and doing what needs to be done.

And sometimes it means stepping back and doing nothing. And that's a whole lot harder.

I put my arm around Ciara's shoulder. "You will never play for him again," I said. "Do you understand?"

"I understand," she said, and started wiping away her tears, and we went to the street and got in a cab.

We didn't say much on the cab ride home. But I thought a lot about what just happened. About what it meant to me as a dad.

You gotta be the kind of dad who will jump into the fray like the mighty man of steel when someone makes your kid cry. That's a given, and I don't care what your philosophy is as a parent, you do what you gotta do. No one makes your kid cry and gets away with it. That's the definition of a Big Daddy right there.

But you also gotta know when to let it be. To let them fall, and pick themselves up, and dust themselves off, and get back in the game. And if you're really good at what you do—if you're really good at being a dad—then by the time they're teenagers they'll have learned a thing or two about how to deal with it all.

Look, in the long run, it was Ciara who hit that kid with a pitch, not the coach. She got that, and she took responsibility for it. I wanted to rip that coach a new one, but Ciara wanted to step up and take the hit. And you know what? If she had struck that kid out and won the game, I wouldn't have been prouder of her than I am right now. And you know what else? I don't think she would be as proud of herself, either. It wasn't easy at the time—but I made damn sure that she understood how proud I was of how she handled herself, and that she should be, too.

And that's another definition of a Big Daddy, too. You might be a crazy lunatic nut job yourself—but you gotta be the crazy lunatic nut job whose kids know, when they do something really, really right, that you're so proud of them you're about to burst.

So I let it go. The cab headed through Midtown, and we looked out the windows, and each of us, silently, said to ourselves, screw 'em. That's just one more thing your kid has to learn to do, sometimes. Just let it go, and move on to the next thing.

And if you can teach your kid that lesson—and learn it yourself—you've done your job for the day.

10

SWEET SIXTEEN AND I DON'T WANNA KNOW ABOUT IT

Now, when I say I don't wanna be a friend to my kids, don't get me wrong. I'm very close with my daughters and I do want them to feel they can come to me with their problems.

Some of their problems, anyway.

Like I said, there are some problems, I'm sorry, that I just don't wanna know about. Like my buddy Willie was telling me. He's driving his daughter to her acting class one day, she's about fourteen, and suddenly she says to him, "Oh my God!"

Girls have a way of saying that, and somehow their moms know exactly what they mean. Girl says, "Oh my God!" and the mom says, "What, you left your book bag at school? There's a history test tomorrow and you need the book so you can study? Why not go over to Sally's house and study with her?" and the girl says, "Sally's got strep." Like she's not even surprised the mom knew exactly what she's thinking.

I think dads shouldn't even try that. They'll just crash and burn. I think you have to fess up immediately. When I have no clue, I say I have no clue. Saves time later.

So my friend Willie's driving with his daughter, and she says, "Oh my God!" and Willie, being the good, smart dad, says, "No clue."

He was about to get one.

"Oh my God," the daughter says. "I forgot a Tampax and I'm wearing white pants and I think I'm about to get my period. What should I do? I don't want to be late. Should I take a chance?"

Now, if there's anyone in the world less qualified to answer that question, it's a dad. How the hell do I know how to figure out the odds on something like that? I think I've established with my daughters that there are certain things you don't talk to Dad about. Anything south of the navel and north of the knees qualifies.

But there are times when you can't avoid it, if you're the dad of teenage girls, and you just have to man up and handle it.

Which comes to our next rule of being a dad. When it comes to figuring out what they're talking about, never fake it—but when they ask for advice, even if it's on something you'd rather take a knee in the balls than talk about—fake it immediately.

Willie flips a coin in his head. It comes out tails. "No worries," he says. Swerves right, pulls in front of their local Duane Reade, double-parks at a hydrant, and hands the girl a twenty. "Go get the Tampax. If you wanna put it in right now, bathroom is in the back on the right. I'll keep the motor running."

My point is, Willie handled the situation like it was a bank robbery. Get in, get the loot, get out. Lots of dads are like that. This one guy I know—I don't want to use his name here, because I don't want to embarrass his daughter—but he's in a meeting and gets a text from his daughter, which says, "My vag is itching. What do I do?"

Thank God it wasn't me. I think I would have just thrown the cell phone out the window and gone back to smoke signals. I don't know. What the hell do you say in a situation like that besides, "Ask your mother"?

The friend takes the safe approach. "Ask your mother," he texts back, and pats himself on the back for a job well done.

"Not home not answering," she texts back.

"Oh shit," he texts back. Not actually, but inside his head. What he does text back is:

"Not sure. I heard of something called Vagisil. Try it."

I don't know how he pulled that out of his ass. If I was on *Jeopardy!* and the category was "Feminine Hygiene Products," I'd just put down the buzzer and walk out of the studio. Fuck it. Maybe that's the answer: If your daughter asks what to do when your "vag" is itching, tell her to call Alex Trebek.

Actually, I gotta hand it to that dad. Not only for having some kind of answer, and not for freaking out the way I would—but for having a relationship with his daughter where she's comfortable to ask him that. That's some special kind of dad.

Not my kind of dad, but special in his own way.

See, when I say I don't wanna be a friend to my kids, I mean, I don't want them to treat me like they treat their friends. I want them to treat me like their dad. Maybe that means I'm not gonna be the best guy to talk about your Tampax issues. But what that also means is, when you need me to have your back, I got your back.

So maybe I'm not exactly your friend. But in a very serious way, maybe I'm the best friend you'll ever have.

Another case in point: There was a teacher in my daughter's class that I started getting a little worried about. She told him one day it was hot in class, and he said, "Well then, take your shirt off." Not a joke you make with a sixteen-year-old girl. I decide to let it go, but I've got my eye on him. Well, a couple weeks later, he passes another remark. My daughter's half Mexican, on Laura's side, and he's Spanish, and the Spaniards tend to look down on

Mexicans, I think. So, she says something in class about not remembering an assignment, and he snaps back, "Well, that's what I'd expect from a Mexican." She comes home in tears.

Now, this is where the Big Daddy comes in.

Because I might not be the guy you can boo-hoo with over a boy who didn't ask you to a party, and I may prefer hitting my thumb with a hammer than hearing about when you're getting your period. But let someone pass a remark about my daughter, and you'll see who's your best friend.

The next day, I call the principal. He sets up a meeting.

I walk into the meeting, and there's the teacher, and I walk up to him slowly and never break eye contact. And I'm just waiting for him to get nasty or make the slightest nod toward getting cocky with me. It's like my right fist is saying, "You know, Steve, we haven't hit anyone in a long time. Don't you think you might let me deck this guy just for old times' sake?" And I'm telling the fist, "Give me just a second, and I'll let you know."

Well, I think the teacher must have overheard the conversation.

The guy is all of five-foot-two, and he weighs about as much as my left ball. He's trembling. He's stammering. I think he's probably pissing his pants, to be honest. The guy is working so hard to apologize, it's pathetic. I hate to say it, but I wanted to just give the guy a hug and say, "There, there, fella, it's gonna be all right." I couldn't even yell at the guy. I just gave him a little pat on the back—a little harder than I had to, maybe, but just to make the point—and said, "Well, let's try to be a little more careful, okay?" And I walked away.

So when I say I don't want to be friends with my kids, understand what I mean. I may not be *that* kind of friend. But when push comes to shove, I'm gonna be their best friend. And they know they can take that to the bank.

What, Exactly, Do You Mean, "He's Just a Friend?"

Now, this whole "friend" question gets really tricky. Because with kids today, they all hang around together, and they all call each other "friends." When I was sixteen, you didn't hang around with girls. You hung around with guys. Girls were for one thing. So I don't quite get this bunch of girls and guys who move in a pack, and all go to dinner and the movies together. It's like some kind of weird group date to me. But my wife assures me that the kids are all just friends.

Once my younger daughter hit sixteen, it became an issue.

Like I said, I'm not the dad they're gonna come to with boy troubles. And that's fine with me. Go ask your mother. You want my advice on boys? Good. Here's my advice. Don't go out with any boys. That's my answer. So like I said, they've learned not to come to me with their boy troubles.

But she starts to like this one boy. He's a nice guy, and very popular. And like I said, they all hang around in a pack, like they're a traveling soccer team on tour or something, you never see one of them without ten of them, but one day, Laura tells me that Josh is coming over.

Josh.

It's the first time, I think, a boy's name is spoken in my home, in relation to my younger daughter, other than when she had a crush on some skinny singer named Sammy Adams. So no big surprise, he accidentally happens to be coming over when I'm out of town. But the next time, he's coming over again, and I'm home.

And I hate this.

Let me tell you something: All dads hate this. They can try to act as cool and mature and with-it as they like. But any dad who pretends he's not freaked out when he meets the first guy who's sweet on his daughter is full of shit.

And I may be a lot of things, but I'm not full of shit.

So everyone in the house knows I'm squirming about this, but they try to make the best of it. And the kid comes over, and he's perfectly sweet and nice and polite. Shakes my hand and looks me in the eye and calls me Mr. Schirripa. I look at him and I call him You Keep Your Fucking Hands Off My Daughter.

Well, not out loud. But you get my drift. I think he probably does, too, but he doesn't show it. He acts like a teenage boy visiting a teenage girl is the most normal thing in the world.

Well, maybe it is. Unless it's *my* daughter.

And there isn't a dad in the world who doesn't think so. And I think if we stopped pretending otherwise, we'd all be a lot better off. You can be the kind of dad who invites the boy to dinner, and encourages the relationship, and all that shit. Or you can be the kind of dad who tells the truth, and says, you want to get to my daughter, you gotta go around me, and trust me, in my case, it's a long way around.

Your choice.

Anyway, they leave, and I'm watching out the window of our apartment. We're high up enough that she can't see me, but as they hit the sidewalk, he puts his arm around her.

And inside, this big tough guy just crumbles. Shatters like a wine glass at a Jewish wedding. Only no one yells, "Mazel tov." It's just you, watching some perfectly nice guy put his arm around your little baby, and you suddenly feel very old.

I don't say anything when she gets back, of course. What are you going to say? "Hi, you know how much of a schmuck your dad can be? Well good, so this won't come as any surprise. I was watching that boy put his hand around your waist, and so now we are flying you to Iceland to live among the monks."

Like I'd even know if there are monks in Iceland, anyway, and if there are, how the hell you'd find them.

So you don't say anything.

When I say you gotta be honest, as a dad, I don't mean *that* honest.

Scare Tactics

See, the thing about being an Italian dad is, what you see is what you get. Or I should say, what you hear is what you get. There's no pretending. There's no layer of sugar coating. My buddy Bill Arnone, the guy I told you about that I met when our daughters were pitching against each other, he's an Italian dad like me. "I always said, 'God help the first boy my daughter brings home,'" Bill said. "You gotta be real special to get anywhere near my daughter. I always told her, bring home a boy you don't like, because he's going to go crawling out of the house crying."

Actually, the first time he saw a boy hanging around his daughter, it was this kid Dante. Bill, to be funny, starts singing a song he made up on the spot, to the tune of "Mambo Italiano." He sings it. "Hey Dan-te, Dante Italiano, hey Dan-te, Dante Italiano." Only at the end, where Rosemary Clooney sings "If you gonna be a square, you ain't a gonna go nowhere," he sings, "If you kiss my daughter, heck, I'm a gonna wring your neck."

The kid, I should point out, was eight years old at the time.

But that's the thing with Italian dads. We are gonna be ridiculously overprotective of our daughters. And proud of it.

"This is who I am," Bill said. "There's no need to interpret. It's all out front." When his daughter makes the mistake of even mentioning a boy to him, he starts scrutinizing the kid like a hawk. Does his daughter appreciate it? Mixed feelings. On the one hand, she appreciates having a dad who is so protective.

On the other, of course, his wife thinks he's crazy.

He has no problem with that.

It's just in our nature to be protective. And that's what it is to be a Big Daddy. Somehow people have forgotten that that's what dads do and that's what dads are supposed to do. When Bill's daughter Allyson went to high school, they lived on Long Island, but she wanted to go to Trinity, a really good prep school in Manhattan. So what does the Big Daddy do? He gets on the 6:45 train with her every morning. Gets off with her at Penn Station. Takes the West Side express up to Ninety-Sixth Street. Walks her to school, then jumps on a bus downtown to get to his office.

Because that's what you do.

After a year or so, she said, Dad, I think I can handle this on my own, I mean, who are you doing this for, you or me?

So he relented.

A little bit at a time.

At first, he only took the train up to Ninety-Sixth Street, crossed the platform, and took the train back downtown. A little while later, he left her at Penn Station.

This is what it is to be a Big Daddy, as your kids get older. You let go, but you hold on, too.

Because that is what you do.

When a Boy Rings the Bell

But to get back to the whole dating thing. I gotta be honest, this was—and still is—my biggest fear. I hate the idea. I just hate it. But the older they get, the more the dating thing starts to become something you have to deal with.

I told you my buddy Anson Williams had a lot to say about what happens when your daughter starts dating. He knows what's what. Because he's speaking from experience.

"I'm the most protective dad in the world," he said. "Because I know guys. And I know guys, because I was there."

Let's be honest, when you're twenty-two years old and starring in a hit TV show like *Happy Days*, it's not exactly tough to attract young females.

"Three weeks before that show started, I was fighting for dates, like every one else," Anson told me. "Then the show hits. You're hot! You're it! People ask me, 'What's the secret to meeting girls?' I tell them, 'You want to know the secret? It's very, very simple. You get on a hit TV show, and you sing. You won't miss.' Three weeks before the show started, I'm a nebbish. Now I'm hot."

But because he was who he was—and because he did stuff we don't exactly have to go into here—now that he's the father of five girls, he's nervous whenever a boy comes to the door.

"Years ago, I'm a cad," he says. "Now, the roles are reversed. I'm answering the door, but I know a lot more than most dads because very few have gone through what I went through with all those girls. So I am so protective. Here's my thing: The nicer the guy is, the more I don't trust him. I'm like, 'Come on, show me who you really are. You're smiling too much. You're too perfect.' I don't like him. I don't trust him."

I'm good with that.

Anson did one other thing that I really like, and that's a really good rule for a Big Daddy.

He made his girls learn the art of self-protection.

Four of them take karate. Three will be black belts within a year; the five-year-old will be a black belt by the time she's nine. This is good for a number of reasons.

One, it teaches them to defend themselves. And also—and a lot of people don't understand this about karate—it teaches them how to respect the people around them and to respect themselves.

But also—and this is the part I like—it gives you something to say to the boys when they show up at your door.

"Hey, welcome!" Anson says he tells the skinny kids who show up to take his precious girls out on a date. "Good to see you! Have fun! By the way"—and here his voice gets really quiet—"she's a black belt. Don't try anything."

Karate, he says, gave his girls confidence. It made them more independent.

Not to mention, if anything happens to Anson, he's got lots of protection.

More Things I'm Not Okay With

Every dad handles the dating thing differently. I have this one friend, he takes the daughter on vacation, she's about sixteen, and the boyfriend comes along. That's okay. And they rent a house in the Caribbean, and that's very okay. And the daughter has her own room, which of course is okay.

And the boyfriend sleeps in the daughter's room. Which is about as far from okay as you can get. I mean, you can start walking around the world, and eventually you're not walking away anymore, you're coming back, and the point where that happens is about as far away from where you started as you can get, and let me say, that doesn't even come close to how far away from okay this dad is when he's letting the boyfriend sleep in the daughter's room.

And for dads who don't want the boy to sleep in the daughter's room, and the mother condones it and says you're being too old-fashioned, and they're going to do it anyway, so better that we should have it under our own roof, and you want to yell and scream about it but you're not sure if it's your place to put your foot down on this one, here's the rule:

Go ahead and yell and scream.

It's okay.

I know everybody doesn't think like me. A good buddy of mine, Charles Tremayne, is a TV producer who came over from England. We argue about this all the time. His daughters are twenty and eighteen now, and he says that if the older one came home with a boy, he'd let them sleep in the same room. He's not sure his wife agrees, and so far the question hasn't come up—but in general, Charles thinks that British parents are more accepting of that sort of thing.

Just one more reason that I'm glad we won the Revolutionary War.

Better It Should Be Under Our Roof?
No, Better It Shouldn't Happen at All

This whole "better it should be under our roof" thing starts with the drinking. I have another friend, his kid is fifteen, he comes home every day and pours himself a rum and Coke, and, being a nice, thoughtful kid, pours one for his dad, and the dad acts like that's the most polite thing he's ever seen and nearly breaks his arm patting himself on the back for raising such a good kid. And when I ask him about it, he says, "Well, they're gonna drink anyway. Better it should be at home, where I can monitor it. And at least they're not driving."

To me, that's setting the bar pretty low. It's like saying, "Yeah, my kid's doing cocaine, but I'm buying it for him, so at least we know it's not cut with rat poison. You know, you get what you pay for."

And I say, that's my point exactly. You get what you pay for. And if you pay for your kids' alcohol because you think it's somehow better than them paying a guy on the street corner to get it for them, then you get exactly what you pay for: a kid who learns that it's okay to get plastered, because Daddy says it's okay.

But you gotta be the Big Daddy. And Big Daddy says it's exactly the opposite of okay.

Look, I've been really lucky. I know how bad it can get. I grew up in an insane house.

One of my sisters would go out drinking, come home at three in the morning, and get into a fight with my mother, that whole scene. I remember lying in bed at three in the morning, listening to everyone screaming and yelling, and there's nothing worse for a kid than that—and there's nothing worse for a dad than that, either. You gotta have rules in your house. Even when they go off to college, you still gotta have rules. My daughter goes off to college, I don't know what goes on, and I don't wanna know. But when she comes home, it's a different story. You're not coming home and staying out until three in the morning and getting loaded. That's just not gonna happen. This is not a dorm room. It's not gonna happen when you're sixteen and it's not gonna happen when you're twenty.

Like I keep saying, you learn the values early and you keep the values late. Whatever you're teaching your kid at sixteen is not about how to get through the next couple of years. It's about how to get through the rest of their life.

And the point is, if you don't want your kid to grow up to be an idiot later, don't let them be an idiot now.

That's not that difficult.

Unless you're an idiot yourself, which, let's face it, most of us can be at one time or another.

Which is why we need the rules in the first place.

More Cool Papas . . .

Among the guys I know, I think that the black dads seem to keep a tighter rein on their kids than the white guys do. The moms, too.

I got a black friend who was pretty wild in his youth, but when he settled down and had a family, he laid down the law. He was very successful and was able to give his kids just about anything they wanted. But he was very strict with them.

I asked him about it and he said, flat out, that people watch black kids more carefully. White kid comes home drunk and annoys the neighbors, people say, well, boys will be boys. Black kid does the same, they say, well, you know how *those* people are. He said that as much as we want to think we're in some kind of "post-racial world," the stereotypes are the same as they always were—and as a black father he has to make sure that his son isn't judged by those stereotypes.

He has no trouble telling his kid, You get on the bus, you come home, you do your homework, you help your mother with the dishes, you turn on the TV after that if you want to, and you get up the next day and do it again. You work hard and you get ahead and you keep your nose clean.

You don't have to like it. But you do have to do it.

If there's a better rule for a Big Daddy to live by, I can't think of it.

. . . And Some Not-So-Cool Papas

But to get back to the question of drinking. It all gets back to trying to be the cool dad. I think it should be clear by now that I have no problem not being the cool dad. I understand why guys want to be the cool dad. Because your dad wasn't, and you want to be different. Because you never grew up yourself, and so when you see the kids hanging around, you want to feel like one of them—or, more important, you want them to feel like you're one of them.

Guess what. You're not one of them. You haven't been one of them in about umpteen-and-a-half years, and you're not gonna get back to being one of them. And, what's a hell of a lot more important than what you might want is what they need. They don't need you to be one of them.

Your kid might hold up one of his friend's parents as the perfect parent because she curses in front of them, or smokes weed, or lets the kids have a beer when they're watching the ball game, or whatever. And you might get jealous because you want to be the one your kid holds up as the great parent instead of some floozy down the street.

Get over it.

Being a good parent is not about being a popular parent. Being a Big Daddy is not about being a popular daddy.

And let me tell you, there's nothing less popular than a parent who goes ballistic the first time you find out your kid had a drink down at the 7-Eleven parking lot.

It's not the popular thing to do. But it's the most important.

One of my daughters got invited to this party when she was about sixteen. Now, as far as I'm concerned, they don't need to go to any parties until sometime around never. And even then, I need to know who the parents are.

I have been convinced by saner minds (which is to say, everybody I know) that you can't just keep them home until they're twenty-one. I still am not sure I understand why, but at the moment I'll accept it. But anyway, in this case, I actually didn't know who the parents were. I made my daughter give me the mom's name and number, and I called her, and told her who I was, and that I just wanted to make sure there'd be some adult supervision at this party.

She never called me back.

So I told my daughter, You're not going.

You can imagine the wailing and screaming and complaining that went on at my house. Pleading, begging, crying, the whole deal. My daughter appealed the case to a higher court (her mom) but was remanded back to the circuit judge (me). I told her, If the mom is so irresponsible that she can't return a simple phone call from the parent of one of her kid's friends, then she's damn well not responsible enough to supervise a party of twenty-four horny teenage boys and giggly teenage girls. I know that for some of those kids the main goal in life is to either get laid, get drunk, or all of the above, and I'm gonna make damn sure there's somebody sane in the house to keep an eye on things.

Here's the kicker: The mom calls us up the next Monday and thanks us for letting Bria come to the party. She didn't even realize Bria wasn't there! We found out the mom spent most of the party down the block at a bar with her boyfriend. This is how she supervises a bunch of teenagers.

Let's face it. At sixteen, the hormones are raging, the desire to experience new things is enormous, and the part of the brain that says, "Um, wait a minute—maybe we ought to stop and think," has not even begun to develop. It's a tiny little surfboard of a thing, and the teenage brain is a hurricane.

So all I'm asking is that some adult is going to act like an adult when teenagers are having a party. And that adult has some sense that it's not okay to give kids alcohol.

Because you know what? A lot of adults don't have that sense. That guy I talked about earlier, who has a rum and Coke with his kid at the end of the day? He's not alone. He's not even unusual. A lot of parents I know say the same thing—they're gonna drink anyway, so I'd rather they do it at home. Why? Because it's so much fun to watch your kid get drunk and throw up? Because you want to make it clear that any behavior is acceptable as long as you tell me about it first? Jesus Christ. What is it with having the kids drink at home? Parents tell me that way they can "supervise" their kids' drinking. Why? What good is that? "Tammy, you know you need to put a lime in that gin and tonic. What were you thinking?" What, you think that if you get your kids to drink with you and you limit it to two drinks, that they'll learn to keep it to two drinks? No. They'll learn that you can't have the third, fourth, fifth, and twelfth drinks until after Daddy has left the room to go watch TV. That's what they'll learn.

The other excuse, of course, is that this way, nobody has to drink and drive. A good goal. You wanna know another way to reach that goal? Nobody drinks! Come on. You know, everybody thinks it's easier now that we've moved to New York City, because at least you don't have to worry that your kid is gonna drink and drive. Because everyone takes the subway or a cab or a car service. But it cuts both ways: Too many parents I know use that as an excuse to give up the responsibility of keeping their kids from drinking, because they say, "Well, how much trouble can they get into? At least nobody's driving."

How much trouble can they get into? Teenagers have little enough sense about how to get through the day without screwing up their lives as it is; give them a couple of drinks, and take away what judgment they have, and you're in deep shit.

But how do you keep kids from drinking? Aren't they going to do it anyway, you say?

You're talking to a book. So how much judgment do you have?

Fortunately, though, there's an answer.

You just gotta be the Big Daddy about it all. My daughters and everyone around them know, if they get caught having a drink, the world will stop turning and everyone will fly off. And that's just for starters.

Does that make me the popular parent? Nope. But does that get in the way of my relationship with my daughters—which, of course, is what everybody is afraid of, which is why most parents don't have the balls to lay down the law?

Nope.

We still have a great time. We still all squeeze together on the couch (because believe me, there isn't a couch big enough that when four of us get on it, and one of them happens to be me, it's not gonna be a tight squeeze) and watch those sappy movies they love (and some not-so-sappy ones, by the way. We watch a lot of those stupid Lifetime movies, we get a kick out of them, but also my kids like the horror movies. I don't like them so much. I actually get scared, frankly. But we have a great time).

My kids and I love each other, pure and simple, and there's nothing in the world that's more important to me than that. I would shove burning coals in my underwear before I'd let anyone hurt them, and they know it. So do they love me back in spite of how strict I am on this? I say they love me *because* of it.

Because they know, somehow, deep in their souls, that the reason I go ballistic on all this shit is because I love them so much it hurts. And that's something every daughter needs to know.

Moms have their own ways of showing daughters their undying, uncompromising, unyielding, unwavering, unconditional love. Girls can yell at their mothers from here until Sunday, and the moms take it, and talk soothingly to them, and they know, both of them, what it really means. Girls yell at their moms, "It's not fair! You're not letting me go to that party and everybody else is going and it's not fair! I hate you!" And the moms will say, "Now, you know why I'm not letting you go, dear. We'll go to the mall instead." And somehow, they both know that that's their way of reassuring each other. The girl knows, I can yell at my mom like that and she will still love me. I can do anything, and my mom will still love me. And that's what girls need to know.

Anybody tries yelling at me like that, of course, they're gonna find themselves locked in their rooms until Obama's grandkids are elected president.

With dads, our daughters may cry and sulk and pout and complain about our rules—but in their hearts, in their souls, they know where their rules come from. If you're fair, if you're not crazy, and you're not strict to the point of being ridiculous, they're gonna know you're making the rules because their dad loves them. And that's what girls need to know, too.

(And just to be clear: I am not fair, I'm fairly crazy, and a lot of times I'm strict to the point of being ridiculous. You don't want to carry the sensible thing too far: Being a little unpredictable makes everybody a little more careful.)

Gotcha

That party where the mother never called me back, and I didn't let my daughter go, wasn't the only party my girls missed on account of me and my rules. I remember this one time, there were these two hotshot parents, both professionals. The party is in Brooklyn. My daughter's a senior in high school. I call up the parents before the party because that's what I do. Like the previous time, I said, if I don't know the parents, I'm at least gonna talk to them.

Now I take it that there's nothing more embarrassing than having your parents call the parents of the kid having a party to find out what's going to happen at that party. I also take it that I don't give a shit how embarrassing it is.

I talk to the dad. I ask, Are you and your wife going to be at the party?

He says, oh yes, we're going to be there all night.

I say, are you going to serve alcohol at this party?

He says, well, we're not going to provide it, but we're not going to police it either. If they bring it in, they bring it in.

Which is about the most asinine thing I've ever heard.

I mean, it's not as bad as some of the parties that were going on—there were parties where the parents actually bought a keg for the kids. Bria, God bless her, is an honest kid, and she always told us when there was a keg at the party. It meant that we watched her like a hawk—but it also meant that she earned our trust.

Until she didn't.

And that's when I learned—when it comes to drinking and partying, it does help to catch your kids messing up one time.

A couple of years back, it was our wedding anniversary, and we decided to go to San Francisco. Great place; my favorite city, outside of New York. Bria was a junior in high school at the time, so we decided to let the girls stay by themselves. One rule: Nobody comes over the house. (Actually there were about ten thousand rules. That's the only one in question at the moment.)

The night we get home, the apartment seems fine, at first glance. But when we looked a little closer, we saw footprints everywhere.

Laura's immediately suspicious. I'm the naive one this time; I'm going, no, they wouldn't have had a party behind our backs. It's too out of character. There must be some explanation.

Laura starts doing a little investigating, talks to the doorman—it never even occurred to us to tell the doorman that no one's allowed over; we didn't even think it was possible that the girls would go behind our backs. That's the kind of relationship we had. Laura makes a couple of calls to some parents, and sure enough, there was a party when we were away.

When Bria got home, I'd like to say I remained calm, cool, and collected. I'd like to say that, of course, except that it's not anywhere close to true.

I was furious. Screaming and yelling like you'd think somebody'd robbed the place. And they had, in a way—because by having that party they'd taken a lot of trust out of that place, and it was gonna be a long time before we got it back. And I made sure, as loudly as possible, that she knew it.

I told her that I had gotten the surveillance tape from the

lobby and that I wanted her to write down the name and phone number of every kid who was at that party, and that I'd know if she left anyone out, and that would make it ten times worse. I didn't actually have the tape, of course, but I never told her that. (Until now, I guess. But hey, you gotta let it go sometime.)

I still have that list, though. It's like a Declaration of Daddyhood—you mess with your father, this is what happens. I wasn't actually gonna call the kids, of course—it wasn't their fault. Someone invites you to a party, you go.

As for Bria, I don't think we could think of enough punishments. We took away everything: the computer, the phone, all of it. She was grounded for eternity plus two weeks.

Because that's what I believe. I've never raised a hand to my kids and never will. But this is what I believe. I'm not a bargainer. I'm not a negotiator. I'm a dad. I'm not unreasonable. I want you to be a nice kid. I want you to be honest. Right, wrong, indifferent, that's just how it is. No one abuses anyone in my house. No one disrespects anyone in my house. And no one lies to anyone in my house.

This is all water under the bridge now, of course. This all happened four years ago.

We're thinking of letting her out of her room any day now.

More Shit I Worry About

Okay, but of all the shit I go through with worrying about my daughters and drinking, then all of a sudden it occurs to you, "What's gonna happen when the idiots around her start drinking?" This is another enormous fear of mine. You ever see these *Jackass* movies? This is another ridiculous cultural event I can't understand for the life of me. These guys do the most disgusting and dangerous stunts known to man—feeding their dicks to a snake, shoving metal dildos up their asses—and things that are ten times more disgusting that I wouldn't even mention. I don't care what these jerk-offs do to themselves. I do care that it became some big phenomenon, three seasons on MTV, three movies (the last one in 3-D, because normal movies weren't disgusting enough for them). I'm not even worried that my kids' friends are gonna try these stunts because my kids are never gonna be hanging around with anybody that stupid.

I do worry that they raise the concept of stupid to a whole new level. If you watch enough of this stuff, you get so used to it, so used to seeing this incredibly over-the-top disgusting behavior, that normal old disgusting behavior doesn't seem so bad anymore. And that's what I worry about: kids getting drunk and just being disgusting. I mean, look, did I used to drink when I was a teenager? Of course. Did I used to chase around after girls when I was drunk? Of course.

Like Anson Williams said, I was there. I know. That's why I'm so protective of my own kids.

But now, you take that testosterone and alcohol, mix them together, and put them out there in a society where you turn on the radio and the top song describes women as "bitches" and "hoes" and includes a detailed description of a blow job, where you turn on the TV and all the reality shows are about acting as disgusting as possible—and then you expect a teenager to figure out what's a normal way to behave? Like I said, I don't worry about my daughters. They're good girls. But I sure as shit worry about the people around them, especially when those people are drunk.

But for all we talk about kids and drinking, that's not even the thing I worry most about.

It's the drugs.

In my world, there weren't a lot of drugs when I was growing up. I know for a lotta guys my age, there was pot, and some other stuff, but for me and the guys I knew, it just wasn't really there.

It's different today. The kids are surrounded by it, and if you don't think so, you're living with your head up your ass. And from what I hear, the drugs are even worse today than they used to be. I wouldn't know, but everybody I know who has smoked pot tells me it's twenty times more potent than it was back when we were kids. Twenty years of experimental gardening, I guess. So even that, I worry about.

You just gotta draw the line. You gotta tell your kids, no matter what other rules I may have for you, and I know I have a lot, this one tops the list. You are not fucking touching drugs. Period. End of story.

I mean, really. Don't be a jackass.

My buddy Charles Tremayne who I told you about, the guy from England, like I said, he's a lot more liberal of a dad than I am. He doesn't worry too much about kids drinking; he doesn't freak out when his daughters start dating.

But here's where even liberal dads from England and crazy Italian dads from Brooklyn agree. Charles has a brother-in-law who has two sons, and he gave the boys the following advice, which Charles stole and gave to his daughters. The rule is: There are three things that will fuck up your life. One, unplanned pregnancy. Two, texting or drinking while you're driving. And three, hard drugs.

I'd add trying to put one over on your father to that list. But for the most part, I'll go along with that.

Still My House, Still My Rules

And you know what? I haven't let up on this, even now when Bria comes home from college. I'm not one of these dads who says,

"You're a grown-up now. You get to play by your own rules." Sorry, but this is still my house, and these are still my rules.

Bria comes home and sees her old high school friends—they're all in college now, too—and all I can say is, whatever lifestyle they're used to at school, it's corrected here. We've had that talk: That's just not gonna fly here. She went to an engagement party. I'm calling and calling her, and there's no answer—you know, she's telling me her cell phone died, the usual bullshit that I have exactly no patience for—and on top of that, she comes home tipsy.

To say that I was unhappy is the understatement of the century.

Laura was out of town—I think she was in Vegas to see her mother—so this one was all on me.

I didn't say anything that night. There's no sense talking in that moment. But the next morning, boy, I let her have it.

I told her, when you get drunk, that's when things happen. That's when things go wrong. That's when God forbid people get raped or get into an accident. That's when the cabdriver takes you where you are not supposed to be. All those things that horrify me. I had all night to imagine all the things that could go wrong, and believe me, I'm really, really good at imagining them, and I laid them all out for her.

Did it do any good? I like to think so. This last summer, she was home, she was working and had to get up early, and God bless her, she hardly went out at all. See, she's maturing. She's figuring it out. I don't have to tell her not to go.

I like to think I helped her learn that already.

I'll tell you one more thing that happens when Bria comes home from school. We all spend time together. Like, Laura and the girls will all go out and get a manicure and pedicure together, and I tell you, these are the things that will stay with them for the rest of their lives. And there's nothing I love more than that. I see a lot of my friends, their kids come home from college, and five minutes later it's, bye. I'm out the door. I'm meeting my friends. See you later.

Not in my house. These kids who don't want to know their parents anymore? I'm not gonna let my kids not know their parents anymore. I am going to be the same Big Daddy I was when they were five: big, loud, and present. Get over here, sit down, we're going out to dinner. Do you have a choice? Absolutely you have a choice. You can get the chicken or the fish.

Whichever you like. You're a grown-up. Who am I to tell you what to do?

You Just Thought of That? Think Again

But there's one last thing you have to worry about when your daughter is old enough to do things that you really don't want her doing. I mean, there's never one last thing—there's always something—but I mean, one last thing I wanna talk about.

I call it the Wild Hair Up the Ass problem.

When we were kids, we'd get a wild hair up our ass to do something stupid. And we'd go do it because there was no one around to stop us. Like I keep saying, why I'm even alive today is a mystery to me sometimes.

So when our daughters get a wild hair up their ass—a sudden urge that they gotta go do something—it's Big Daddy's job to say, "No, you actually don't have to go do that thing. You don't have to do anything. Except calm the fuck down."

My kids are good kids, but they're always taking shots. My younger daughter announces the other night, out of nowhere, that some friend called, and they're all going to Union Square for yogurt. Guess what? No, you're not going to Union Square for yogurt. Why? Two reasons. One, I said so. Two, gimme a minute, I'll think of another reason. In the meantime, stay with Reason One.

You want a reason? I'll give you a reason. Because that's no place for a young girl to be at eleven o'clock at night. Nothing but trouble is waiting out there. Okay, maybe trouble and yogurt. But that's about it, and the yogurt's not worth the trouble. You wanna plan ahead? You want to do something with your friends? We'll talk it over with the parents, decide whether one of us should come with you, that's one thing. You wanna announce a Chinese fire drill and everybody's running out of every door like a chicken with its head cut off, that's something else.

I see these kids, out there on the subway, eleven o'clock at night, I think, what the hell are the parents thinking? I was on the subway the other night. There's this scumbag there with two big bamboo sticks. What the hell is he doing with those sticks? I got no idea, but I don't think he's gonna start clicking them together and singing "Kumbaya." These other guys on the train, you can tell, they're just looking around for trouble. I'm a great big guy and they're probably not gonna mess with me, but a couple of teenage girls out on their own? Forget about it. And it's not just New York, and it's not just the subway. It's everywhere.

And it's not just about the danger, either. It's about the tough concept that you gotta teach your kid, because their brain isn't developed enough to grasp the concept on their own. Which is the idea that maybe you gotta think before you act. That maybe you don't give in to every harebrained thought that comes into your head or into your friends' head. That when somebody says jump, you maybe don't jump right away. This is something your kid needs to know, because at some point she's gonna leave home and somebody's gonna suggest some leaps that you really need her to look before she takes. There are gonna be bigger mistakes to make than going to Union Square at eleven o'clock at night, and at some point they gotta start recognizing them.

Until then, it's a dad's job to point out to kids when they have a bad idea. You wanna change your name to Void? Brilliant. Now no one could ever write you a check. You wanna name your band The Pot Is in the Glove Compartment Behind the User's Manual? Brilliant.

You just don't do some things. Once in a while you can let them make a mistake and learn from it. Sometimes you just gotta say, I'm your father, and I love you, so do me a favor on this particular day and don't be an idiot.

And in the meantime, put some yogurt in the fridge and save everybody a lot of heartache.

Big Daddy Holiday: "Don't Teach Your Daughter to Drive Day"

When I say I'm the luckiest guy in the world, I mean it in a lot of ways, and one of those is: Both of my kids just flunked their driving tests.

I know that sounds harsh. But you know what?

When you're an overprotective, worrying dad like me—like any self-respecting Big Daddy—there's just so many things you can worry about at once. I'm not that smart that I can hold ten fears in my head at the same time. I forget which one to worry about first. So if you can take one off the table for me, that's a good thing. I wish they never learned to drive. But I know that's ridiculous.

I also know, sometimes there's nothing wrong with being ridiculous.

Being New Yorkers, it's not as big a deal, because most New York kids don't drive. But at some point, I know, I'm gonna have to deal with it.

So, I feel sorry for the girls that they flunked their driving tests. Bria wasn't in a hurry—she's twenty and just got around to taking it—Ciara took it three days after she turned seventeen.

Bria's not too sad about it. Ciara's much more unhappy. I'm sorry for her, but I don't pretend that I'm unhappy that I don't have to worry about them driving, even if it's just for a little while longer.

Me, I got my license in high school, the way a lot of my friends did. There was this guy named Ed, who was the driver's ed teacher and the gym teacher. And you paid him two hundred bucks, and you got your blue card that says you passed the course. And that's what you needed to get your license.

I know that option is off the table. For one thing, I don't even know where Ed lives anymore.

I wasn't the one who taught my daughters to drive, by the way. There was not a chance of that happening. I wasn't gonna do it, and there's no way they were gonna let me.

I'm not that good a driver anyway, to be honest. I'm better than Laura says I am, or than the girls think I am, but I'm not that great. But that's not the problem. The problem is, I'd be so fucking nervous with the girls behind the wheel. There's no way I could possibly teach them to drive. I'd make them crazy. I'd be hanging out the window, screaming at everybody on the street, "Look out! Look out! A kid is driving! Get out of the way!"

This, I'm pretty sure, would not give them the confidence they need.

FOR LITTLE GIRLS GET BIGGER EVERY DAY

There are two words that no father ever wants to hear, when it comes to your daughter.

Birth control.

Separately, those words are fine. Birth? Good thing. Glad you were born. Control? I definitely am in favor of control, and if I'm the one who's in control, even better.

But put them together, and they conjure up images no father ever wants to think of. It's making me nauseous just talking about how I don't want to talk about it.

This one friend of mine told me his older daughter had a case of acne at school, and at one point it got bad enough that they had to put her on medicine, and part of the medicine was that she had to take birth control pills. It helped regulate the hormones, or something.

At least, that's what they told him. His wife said, That's why she's on the birth control. You know what? He was so happy to believe that, it's ridiculous. Good for him. I'm on his side.

Another guy I know, same thing. His daughter went to college, started having some emotional problems with the whole withdrawal from the family thing. So they put her on some medication, Prozac or whatever, but they also put her on birth control pills, because they said that would keep her more emotionally stable. Again, I know I could probably find out in two seconds if that's even possible or true. And again, that's two seconds I absolutely have no reason to spend.

Every dad should pray for this. That they find some other reason for your daughter to go on birth control, so that (a) she's on birth control, for Chrissakes, so that if anything should, you know, happen, she's protected, which is a good thing, and (b) you can pretend that nothing is, in fact, you know, happening, which is an even better thing.

Because if your kid is a normal kid, then at some point, things are going to progress past the stage of holding hands with her boyfriend on the way back from the movies. Past the stage of kissing good night. Past the stage of, if I have to think of one more thing that's past that stage, I'm seriously going to have a heart attack.

Because that's the hardest part of being a Big Daddy. Is that one day your little girl is gonna grow up. And you want that. You want her to be strong and independent and happy and in control and confident, and all that.

And along with all that comes the thing that no Big Daddy can talk about when it comes to his little girl. In the old days, this is something that dads didn't talk to their daughters about. Only moms.

Which works for me just fine.

This one dad I know, he has four girls. He insisted that they go on birth control, each of them, when they turned sixteen. For me, this guy goes in the category of dads who need to be slapped. I think he's a total whack job. What kind of message are you sending your daughters, that now it's okay to go out and have sex with some guy? Give me a break.

As for my kids and birth control: I got no idea, I don't want to have any idea, and if they are reading this and wonder if they should tell me, let me take a second and say, really, no. Go on to the next thing.

Because I'll be honest, when it comes to boys around my daughters, I just don't want to think about it and I don't think there's anything wrong with not wanting to think about it. That's one thing that I think they had right in my parents' generation: Girls talked to their moms about this stuff. Not their dads.

I just don't want to know. I mean, I know what I did when I was a kid. Sometimes I think having two daughters is my payback for that. My older one, I don't even want to see her kiss a guy, and she's turning twenty-one. I see them holding hands, that's enough for me. I get the picture. She's dating a nice guy now, a little older. Came here, shook my hand, looked me in the eye, I'm good with that. But that's about all I'm good at. I mean, it was not that long ago that she was a baby. And then she's dating a kid in high school, what do you think he's thinking about? (Like I said, don't answer that.)

Because this is another rule I live by: Dads think differently about boys than they do about girls, and there's nothing wrong with that. I know the cool thing these days, the popular thing, is to treat girls equally. But on this subject, I just can't do it. I just can't.

Look, this guy I know, he has two sons. He's telling me that his boys go to Florida on spring break, and they're fucking everything that walks, and he's bragging about it like it's a great thing. "Don't let your daughters go to Florida," he tells me. "My kids are fucking everything down there."

First off, other than wanting to punch this guy in the throat for even talking about my daughters that way, I'm thinking, What a moron you are! You're proud of the fact that your kids are fucking lots of girls? This is a thing to be proud of? This is what's wrong—parents have lost any perspective on the values they're teaching these kids. Everywhere you look. You watch *Glee*? Everybody's fucking. You listen to music? All about fucking. Now, in this environment, my daughter wants to go meet a boy, I'm gonna be comfortable about that?

No fucking way.

I've said it many times and I'll say it again, I never wanted a boy, we never tried for a boy, there's a different set of problems with a boy—but this is one problem you don't have with a boy.

And here's another. I think that with a boy, you love him, but when he goes, he goes. He goes into the army, he goes out into the world, he gets a job, he's a man. With a girl, you never stop worrying. What if she marries the wrong guy? What if she wants to work but he doesn't want her to? What if she doesn't work but then he can't support her? Is he gonna take care of her like we do? For Chrissakes, what if she marries a guy who's violent? How will I know? What if she doesn't tell me? What if he cheats on her and she finds out? What if he cheats on her and she doesn't find out?

You can tell me that there are fears with boys when they go out in the world, too, and I'll believe you. But you can't tell me they're as great or as terrifying or as horrible as the fears I have for my daughters. And if you wanna call me sexist for thinking that, then go ahead, but I'm gonna worry about my daughters forever. Because that's what Big Daddies do.

Big Daddy's Little Girl

You know what commercial chokes me up? There's this dad, talking to his little girl. She's maybe seven years old, and she's sitting

behind the wheel of a car. He's looking in the window, saying, okay, this is your first time driving alone; check your mirrors, and be extra careful getting on the highway, and all that. They cut away to the dad, and then back to the girl, and you see she's really a teenager. Only before you were seeing her through the dad's eyes and she was just seven years old.

Seen this commercial a hundred times, and it always gets to me. You know why? Because that's exactly what it means to be a Big Daddy. It's about the fact that no matter how old they get, they're always gonna be your little girl. And you're always gonna wanna watch out for them.

Which gets really, really tough, when they're finally ready to leave home.

I remember when Bria went to college. First of all, she wanted to go away, and I wanted her to go. I never got the chance to go away to college, and I think when you go away it helps you grow up. You have to do your own laundry, no one's waking you up to go to school, no one's telling you to do your homework. This is the first step to taking responsibility for yourself. You're there because you wanna be there. So we had the conversation with her: You don't have to go. You can stay home and go to college. Or you can not even go to college now. But if you go, it's because you want to.

Laura did most of the college search trips—I went on maybe two of them. I did help her out with the interviews, though. I made sure she got the interviews because she's one of these people who comes off much better in person than she does on paper. Some people are better on paper: You look at some kid's résumé, and you think, man, this kid has really got it together; and then you meet the kid, and he can barely fucking speak, can't look you in the eye, and doesn't seem to have taken a shower since the last time the Mets were in the World Series.

At one of the schools she applied to, one of the ones she really liked, Bria got an interview with the admissions office. I went along for this ride, and on the way I just kept telling her: Be honest. Be yourself. Don't try to make yourself something you're not. Just be who you are.

Well, she listened to me all right.

Maybe a little too carefully.

She gets into the room, and she's in there for like forty minutes. I know that's a long time for a college interview, so I wonder what the hell is going on.

When she comes out, the admissions officer starts telling me what a wonderful girl she is, and I just about wanted to cry. Someone who just met her, and is telling me how great she is, all these nice things. That's all a dad ever wants to hear.

"I asked her, 'What is the one thing no one knows about you?'" the admissions officer told me. And you know what Bria told him? She said, "I try and try. And no matter how hard I try, I cannot do better in school."

My heart sank. When I told her to be honest, did she have to be *that* honest?

Turns out she did. She got into the school.

She's on the Dean's List now, by the way.

When I think back on it, I think, that was a pretty ballsy thing she did, telling the admissions officer what she told him. And that's what I hope they learned from their Big Daddy. With me, what you see is what you get. Like it or not, this is it. That's the one thing I've told them all their lives. That's the one thing I tried to instill in them.

And sometimes, just sometimes, I think it might have stuck.

Which matters a whole lot.

Because look, I kid around a lot, and I go crazy a lot, but if you want to be serious, I will say it straight out: My kids, and my wife, are my whole life. I would have gone off the rails a long time ago if it wasn't for them. The acting thing, everything else—that's what I do. But it's not who I am. My family—that's who I am, and that's why I am. End of story. When the four of us are together, that's the only time I'm truly at peace. They are like air to me—I would have been gone a long time ago if I didn't have them to give my life purpose and meaning.

So yeah, I hold my breath a lot when it comes to moments like this—moments that are gonna define their lives. And yeah, I breathe a big sigh of relief when these moments come out okay.

It's not like I don't care about anything else—I care about a lot of shit. I care about my next job. I care about whether the place I get shrimp from is open late tonight. I care about whether the Knicks are gonna collapse again.

But compared to my family—nothing means anything to me.

Because they mean everything to me.

It's that simple.

In the End, I Still Gotta Be Me, You Still Gotta Be You

I was thrilled when Bria got accepted, but right away this whole new set of worries that come with sending a kid off to college came flooding in. I've heard it from a lot of my friends—there are a whole lot of other challenges that rise up when your kids go away to college. So that's a whole new set of rules for the Big Daddy to make up as he goes along.

For example, this guy Matty I know, a stockbroker who commutes in from Connecticut, he faced the hardest challenge a dad ever faces.

Because his daughter, his beautiful, precious daughter, his wonderful perfect daughter, who is all of twenty-one and getting ready to start her senior year in college, calls him up one day, and says, me and my boyfriend are thinking of moving in together, and how do you guys feel about that?

His first thought, of course, like any dad, is: Holy shit! I will kill him and burn his body and spread the ashes over the Gowanus Canal before I let some douche bag move in with my daughter.

Fortunately, he doesn't say that.

His second thought, like any dad, is: Holy shit! My wife's not home. I gotta make the call on what to say here. I'm out here flying solo, and I can barely read the instruments on this fucking plane, and is that a mountain I'm about to crash into or is my life flashing before my eyes just for the hell of it?

Fortunately, he doesn't say that either.

What he does say, which is what guys like him are trained to say—well-educated, well-off, upper-middle-class liberal kinds of guys, is: "Well, dear, there's a lot that goes into this decision. Have you thought about how the finances would work, and all that?"

He's stalling, see. I mean, he's met the boyfriend: nice enough guy, been over the house to dinner a couple of times, but not the sharpest knife in the drawer. And he knows his daughter pretty well, too: She's been dating guys since she's fifteen; she's as cute as cute can get, so she attracts them like flies, and she goes for guys who are pretty good-looking and fun, if not the most ambitious. So Matty's always been cautious. Still, he never prepared for this moment. So he's stalling for time. He's looking around the kitchen while he's on the phone, like maybe the wife left him instructions on "what to do if your daughter says she wants to move in with somebody."

But there are no instructions.

So he has to wing it.

He stays on the details for a while: He talks about how it would be better if the apartment is in her name, instead of his, so if things don't work out she doesn't have to move. He asks her why they're thinking of doing this, and she says, "Well, we don't get to see each other enough because of our schedules, so this would make things a lot easier."

This, he thinks, is a pretty shitty reason to move in together.

Unfortunately, he does not say this.

What he does say is, "Look. You're a grown woman. You're twenty-one. This is your decision, and whatever you decide I'll support you one hundred percent. I just want you to realize that this is a big decision, and it could turn sour, and that will be tough."

Bzzzzt! Wrong answer.

He hangs up, and immediately starts feeling nauseous. Shit! His baby is moving in with a guy. She has no idea how huge this is. And he didn't say a word to stop her.

He feels a little better when the wife comes home and pretty much agrees with what he said to his daughter. She praises him for being so calm and rational. They call the daughter back that night and get on both extensions, and pretty much go over the same ground.

But the next morning, something happens. Something snaps in his brain.

I think maybe he finally started channeling his inner Big Daddy.

He calls her back.

"Look," he says. "I thought about what I said last night and I want to take back some of what I said. Honestly, I've been thinking about all of this and, honestly, to tell you how I feel, I do not think it is the right thing to do. I know that this might make me sound really old, but this is a huge step. Remember when you were a kid and you learned the phrase 'this shit is serious,' and we tried to get you not to use it, but you did all the time anyway? Well, guess what.

"This shit is serious."

There was silence on the phone, and he felt like he'd just jumped out of that plane without a parachute. But when you jump out of a plane without a parachute, there's nothing really to do but keep going in the direction you're going and hope you get really lucky and hit a haystack.

"Moving in together is like getting married," he told her. "You guys don't realize how young you are and how tough this is. But look. If you really love this guy so much, you need to see him every single morning the second you wake up, and feel lovesick when he's not around, and really are ready to fight through all the fights that happen when you live together because you love each other that much, then maybe. But otherwise, don't even think about it. It's just too big a deal."

Again, silence.

"I'm sorry," he said, "but I thought I owed it to you to tell you how I really felt."

He heard his daughter's voice on the other end.

"Thank you," she said. "I think I really needed to hear that."

Whattaya know. Landed on a haystack after all.

Within a couple of days, the kids decided not to move in together. Within a couple of weeks, they weren't a couple anymore. A few weeks later, she starts dating another guy. Not nearly as good-looking. But he owns his own business already and is applying to law school.

Not that that's what's important, obviously.

What's important is this:

If you got anything out of this book, other than a couple of laughs, I hope it's that being a Big Daddy is not the most popular thing you can do these days. It's not the way everybody says you're supposed to be.

In the end, I call 'em like I see 'em. Just like my friend Matty did.

And that's what being a Big Daddy is all about.

Letting Go

But still, I know that when your kids go off to college, you have to let go. A little. I told you my buddy Charles Tremayne is a lot more liberal than me. He's helping me through this whole idea of letting go. (Right now his daughter is hiking through the Himalayas as we speak. He told me she's with a group, so she has protection. I'm thinking, With a group? A group of what? If she was with a group of super FBI agents and NYPD cops, maybe that might be enough protection for me. My daughter's getting ready to travel soon, so I gotta figure out how to handle this in a calm way, maybe a little more like Charles does.)

Charles says it's a cultural thing. "From England, it's a different perspective. I think that there's always been that traditional thing where we let our kids fly as soon as they can. Americans in general are more overprotective than Brits. In Britain, you're happy to have them going around on the tube—the subway—at a young age. Here, you worry about it more."

Well, you got that right. I'm worried about his daughter already. And get this: On Charles's kid's trip, they even take away their cell phones, to get them totally involved in where they are. He hasn't talked to his daughter for weeks.

Talk about a better man than I am. That would drive me nuts. I'm thinking of suggesting to my daughter that if she wants to travel, maybe she could do it without actually leaving town. I know that doesn't make much sense, but I'm working on it. Give me a little time.

She's Leaving Home

My buddy Bill Arnone, the lawyer, just sent his daughter off to college. They visited twenty schools before she picked one. Twenty! And he was there every step of the way. One thing he noticed, though, which is a great tip for dads when their daughters are ready to pick a school: Never, ever tell them which one is your favorite. It's the kiss of death. Bill was a Jesuit college kid himself, so he was rooting for one of those. "I told her my favorite was Georgetown," he said. "It dropped to the bottom of her list like a rock. That's the thing with girls. It goes both ways. They want your approval. But they also have a need to rebel. So you have to watch that."

With us, like I said, it was Laura who made most of the college visits with Bria. I was involved some. But I gotta say, for all the months and months of preparation and horror stories from my friends, it didn't really, really hit me until we were driving her to college, a couple of hours away, that she was actually leaving home. Suddenly, I have this really sick feeling in my stomach. For real, like somebody punched me in the gut. We get there, and all these kids are moving into the dorms, and chattering away, and we're helping her set up her room, and swear to God, I think I'm gonna puke.

Bria didn't have any roommates that first year, which I think was a good thing. I know they say, you're away from home and it's good to have roommates because suddenly you have these instant friends, but I only think the other way. I think, what if you get a whacko who's homesick and whatnot, and now you're not only worrying about school but you're worrying about some screwball roommate who doesn't have her act together? That's how my mind works. I'm always searching for the disaster that's about to happen around my kid, and trying to figure out how to prevent it. It's like

I'm walking through life with a nail gun in my pocket and some two-by-fours in the truck, so I'm ready to shore things up in case the walls start crumbling down around my kids. That's what Big Daddys do. We hunt for disasters like a caveman looking for mastodons. Or whatever cavemen did to protect their kids. What the fuck do I know? Do I look like a history teacher to you?

She met some kids in the hall, and they all started talking about going down to scope out the cafeteria, and so Laura and I figured it was time to leave.

And I wanna tell you, this is the hardest thing I ever had to do in my life.

I remembered, suddenly, this moment when she was a little girl. She never went to preschool, so kindergarten was the first time she was away from us. And she didn't want to go, and every day for two weeks she'd cry when we left.

And I looked at my little girl, standing there, in the dorm room where we were about to leave her, and drive away. And suddenly she was five years old. And there was no teacher there to distract her with toys, no little kids running around making noise. She was just standing there, looking at me. Looking at me getting ready to leave her.

And I started bawling like a baby.

I grabbed her, and hugged her, and she was crying, too, and so was Laura. And then I did the hardest thing.

I let her go.

I let her go, and Laura and I went back to the car and started driving home. We had made a deal with Bria that she wouldn't come home for the first month. Because if you start getting into that routine where you are coming home every weekend, you don't make friends, and that makes it worse. So we had made it that she'd stay at school for at least a month before she came home.

It was a long month. Even though she was just a couple of hours away, it felt like she was out in outer space. She made friends at school—she makes friends easily—but when she finally did come home, she started feeling a little homesick. She said, "Maybe I should come back home and go to school here." We talked it over, and I gotta say, for a guy who doesn't have enough patience to fill a thimble, I was pretty patient about this one. I wanted to start to grill her—Why, did something happen in school? Is somebody being an asshole? Tell me who it is, I'll kill them!—but I decided, for once, let's just let it ride, for a bit. For once, Big Daddy's not gonna come storming in to fix things. I'm just gonna sit back and see what happens.

Even Big Daddies have to let go, sometimes.

I'm not sure when it happened, but it was pretty soon after that that Bria stopped talking about coming home to live again. In fact, she stopped coming home altogether! We had to tell her to come home. I think she was having so much fun, she just kind of got caught up in things.

Laura and Bria still talk and text just about every day. And last week, I hear a key in the door, and I think it's Laura, and I look up—and it's Bria! Came home from college on a Saturday morning, just to surprise us. No reason. See her sister play ball, give her Big Daddy a hug.

That, my friends, is what it's all about.

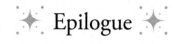 Epilogue

STEVE'S PEEVES

Now I know that up to this point I have been maybe a little shy about expressing my point of view. What can I say? I'm a naturally quiet person. A big pussycat. Just ask anyone.

Well, not my kids. Or my wife. Or the doorman in my building. Or most of my friends. Or anyone I work with, or have ever worked with, or have ever met. But I mean, anyone else.

So before we finish up, I gotta get a few more things off my chest. These are my top pet peeves when it comes to parents and their kids.

1. YOUR KID IS NUTS. DEAL WITH IT.

What is it with these parents who let their kids run wild? I see it every step of my day.

Get in the elevator in the morning. There's this kid, he

loves to push every button in the elevator. The mom, in the sweetest tone, tells her, "Now dear, remember, we don't press all the elevator buttons?" Well, clearly we don't remember that. Maybe if you reacted like you didn't think this is the cutest thing in the world, she'd remember. Look, I get that the kid is curious, but just because they're little doesn't mean they don't know what's going on. They're trying to manipulate you and figure out where the limits are. Clearly, the limit for this kid is somewhere up near where the Mars Rover landed. Just because they named the thing Curiosity doesn't mean that the sky's the limit.

Next stop, the front lobby. I got one family in my building, the kid comes downstairs with his scooter, he's riding the scooter around the goddamn lobby while the parents are chatting with the guy at the front desk. You know, instead of saying what any normal person should be saying in that situation, which is, "Get off that scooter! What are you, crazy? Who does such a thing?" they say, "Well, this is part of his learning experience. He has to learn to express himself. Some of that expression is nonverbal." I'll give you a nonverbal expression, lady, only I'm polite enough not to flip you the bird in front of your kid.

I already talked about what goes on in the restaurant. That's the worst. For a lot of kids, that's the one place they spend some time where they're expected to act like normal human beings. Not monkeys. The restaurant is a good place to teach your kid the theory of evolution—that we have evolved from apes and aren't supposed to act like them anymore. Most restaurants, you look around, and you want to say, Where the hell is Charles Darwin when we need him? Because these kids seem to be evolving back.

2. PARENTS WHO MAKE THEIR KIDS PERFORM.

So, I get that the parents can't stop the kids from acting like monkeys. But do they have to make them perform like monkeys, too?

It drives me nuts. Whenever you go over some people's houses, they gotta make the kid perform. Kid is learning the violin, the piano, good for him. Like I said, it's important to expose your kids to a lot of things. You just don't need to expose the rest of us to it while you're in the process.

Five minutes in the house, and it's, oh, you have to hear Johnny play the Moonlight Sonata. Johnny, play the Moonlight Sonata for Mr. Schirripa. And the kid, of course, hates this, and says no. Now, I don't know who's pissing me off more at this moment—the mom for forcing the kid to perform, which I don't wanna hear because what the fuck is the Moonlight Sonata anyway? What, I got up in the morning and said, you know, my day's not gonna be complete unless I hear a seven-year-old banging out Beethoven or whoever the fuck it is on an out-of-tune piano? Or the kid, who seems to think it's okay to say no to her mother like she was talking to the dog. Or the mom again for not noticing that the kid is talking to her like the dog. "Please, sweetie, play just the first part, and then you can go watch TV with some ice cream." Okay, now the mom is bribing the kid. This is a brilliant strategy. Not only are you teaching the kid not to do what you say, but you're rewarding the kid with ice cream for being obnoxious. Who the hell is in charge of this situation?

You know this is not for the kid's benefit anyway. And it's sure not for mine. Let's face it, this is for the parent's benefit. Look at what a good parent I am, my kid has piano lessons on Monday, singing lessons on Tuesday, she's shooting a commercial on Wednesday, I'm taking her to Paris on Thursday, I'm giving her a Ferrari on Friday. We haven't planned the weekend yet. I like to be spontaneous.

So now the mom and the kid bargain awhile, and I wanna say, Look, kid doesn't want to play Moonlight Sonata, I'll live, really. I'll go buy the CD later. I'll listen in the car on the way home. Better idea! I'll go home and listen to it right now, while you guys work this out!

But no go. I gotta sit there and watch this mother plead with her daughter to play. Finally, the daughter relents, and slumps over to the piano, and plays the first nine notes, and gets it wrong at the end, and says, "No, wait." And she starts again, and gets it wrong again, and says, "No, wait," and I feel like I'm trapped in some goddamned time warp, and I'm gonna spend the rest of my life watching this kid hunt for that note.

So do me a favor. You wanna teach your kid to play the piano, fine. You want me to hear it? Wait 'til she grows up and plays Carnegie Hall, and send me two tickets. I won't go, of course, but my wife and daughters will, and they'll come tell me how good it was. I promise.

3. PRIVILEGED KIDS ACTING LIKE OVERPRIVILEGED KIDS.

I said before, in my line of business you run into a lot of rich guys, and for some reason, when it's their kids who are being the jerks, it pisses me off twice as much. Not that their kids are that much more badly behaved (although a lot of them are), but because these are the people who have the resources to get some help, to raise their kids right—they're not working two jobs to pay the rent, they're not coming home dead tired from being on their feet all day, they're not spending the weekend catching up on the laundry and repairing a hole in the ceiling where there was a leak from the bathtub in the apartment above. They have people to do all that shit so they can spend time with their kids. I give a lot of parents a break because I know how tough it can be—but these rich folks who don't discipline their kids, that gets under my skin.

Case in point. I was at Yankee Stadium the other day. Great seats, second row behind home plate, courtesy of a friend of mine. Sitting right in front of us is this guy with two kids. Clearly the guy's got money; they're in the front row, and those seats cost like $1,200. One kid is a lunatic. Banging on the chair, standing up right in front of us. The dad, texting on his iPhone, doesn't tell the kid to sit down. Finally, I tap the kid on the shoulder and say, nice and friendly, "Hey, down in front, pal," and the kid ignores me like maybe the wind was blowing from behind him. Just turns away. I know the dad heard me, but he ignores the whole thing. Now Derek Jeter is in the on-deck circle, and the kid starts yelling, "Jeter! Jeter! Jeter!"—trying to get his attention. Real obnoxious, like he expects that Jeter should turn around. Not nice, not polite—a really shitty tone of voice. Does it for every single batter! "Granderson! Granderson! Granderson!" like the kid is George Fucking Steinbrenner and he wants to chew the guy out for being late to practice.

Down in those seats, you don't pay for anything, so when the waitress comes around, this guy's kids just turn to him and say, "Ice cream! We want ice cream!" Could you just slap those kids? Not "Can I have an ice cream, please" or anything like that. And when the guy comes back, the kids just start yelling, "Gimme! Gimme!"

I tell you what. My kid ever yells "Gimme gimme" to me,

I'll give them something. Something to remember. Good thing they never tested me on that one.

And again—just the other day, I'm in the lounge at the airport. I'm stuck there for eight hours. There's two mothers there, two blondes, drinking fucking white wine. They've got three little kids, they've spread out a blanket, they have clothes, the bassinet, the whole nine yards. I'm thinking, What are they doing, sitting there drinking wine while the kids are tearing up the fucking joint? I came this close to saying to them, Are you fucking kidding me? Is this necessary? And the drinking irritates me. Can you handle the kids better drinking white wine? It just fucking amazes me.

4. PARENTS WHO NEED TO BE SLAPPED.

Some parents are so ridiculous, they drive me nuts. These are some parents who need to be slapped:

- Parents who take their baby to the movies and don't leave when the kid starts crying, like maybe it improves the soundtrack.

- Parents who think their kids are gifted when they're barely above being morons themselves.

- Parents at sporting events whose asses are on the sidelines but whose mouths are on the field.

- Lindsey Lohan's parents.

- Anyone who puts their kids in a reality show or lets them watch one.

- Parents who send tweets as if their baby wrote them. Twits.

- Kim Kardashian's parents.

- Parents who hire a "parenting coach" to teach them how to be better parents. I swear to God I just saw this advertised in the *Post*. Are you kidding me?

- Parents who send me letters at Christmas telling me what their families did the past year. Unless you're going into the Witness Protection Program and this is the last time I'll hear from you, I don't give a crap.

- The Utah mother who allowed her children to use a portable potty in the middle of a restaurant (true story—you can't make up people like that).

- Parents who spend $1,000 on a stroller, then have their $12-an-hour nanny push it around.

- Parents who don't let their kids eat any sugar but feed them prescription drugs like they're M&Ms.

- Parents who let their kids play video games all day long, then wonder why their kids are antisocial.

- Parents who buy their twelve-year-old daughter a handbag that you'd need a bank loan to afford.

- Parents who let their dogs run free but keep their kids on a leash.

5. WE INTERRUPT THIS LIST FOR AN IMPORTANT MESSAGE.

Here's another thing that makes me nuts. Kids who—wait a second—are constantly—I said wait a second, did you hear me say wait a second?—kids who—really, when I say wait I mean wait!—interrupting.

You know, when we were growing up, they said kids should be seen and not heard. I don't believe that, and nobody does anymore. But there's a time and a place. And when your dad is talking to someone, that's not the time or the place. Unless it involves blood, flames, or asphyxiation, it can wait until I'm done talking.

Is it hard for kids to learn how to time an "excuse me" for when somebody's finishing up a thought? No doubt. Is this a skill that might be useful to them (more so than, oh, I don't know, playing the Moonlight Fucking Sonata)? No doubt.

I'm talking to this buddy of mine, just the other day, and the kid—not a toddler, mind you, this kid is like eight years old already—won't stop talking. Jabbering away, pulling the dad's sleeve. Dad is trying to ignore the kid. Finally, he says, "Just wait a minute, buddy," which affects the kid the way a ceiling fan affects a bowling ball. Grabbing, pulling, yakking. I feel like telling the dad, "Listen, your story is very interesting. Why don't you pause it and come back and tell me the rest when your kid is like maybe twenty-five and living in your basement?"

But you know who I feel most sorry for in this situation (outside of me, of course)? It's the kids' teachers. I was at a back-to-school night one time, when the girls were little, and the principal was begging the parents. She said, your kids are teacher-deaf, and they're teacher-deaf because they're mommy-deaf and daddy-deaf. What she meant was, she watches how the parents are with their kids, and when the parents tell the kids to quiet down, and the kids ignore them, the parents just don't react. It's like they're blind, deaf, and dumb.

How are these teachers supposed to control twenty-five of these kids when the parents can't control one of them? I mean, I'm not saying you should make your kid sit up straight at the table and if they speak out of turn you should rap their knuckles with a ruler. Far from it.

The back of your fork will do just fine.

The other part of this that drives me nuts is that when the kid has something to say, they expect the whole world is gonna stop for whatever lamebrain idea has just come in their head. Laura and I are getting ready for dinner one night, and Ciara comes in and announces, "I want to go to a concert." Okay, great. I'll alert the media at once. Who the hell taught you that we're all going to drop everything the moment you have a desire to do something? Must be the parents in your secret other life, because it certainly wasn't us. One, I'm busy. Two, we have to figure this out. What concert? Who's going? How are you gonna get there? Who's paying for this? What night is it? What are me and your mother doing that night?

That's another thing. When I'm out to dinner, or whatever, I want to know that the kids are home and safe. I don't need to be worrying about them. You wanna go to a concert, I wanna be home that night, ready to roll, so that if anything goes wrong, I'm there. That's what I like to do. And when I'm out, I wanna know that the kids are home, and that they're not putting anything in the oven they're going to forget about and somehow involve municipal workers in uniform opening the front door with an ax. I don't wanna worry about where you are at ten o'clock, where you are at midnight, whether you got a cab, nothing. You have a nice TV, you have a nice apartment, you can suffer there for one night.

So like I said, when the kid walks in the room and interrupts everybody and announces their plans, you gotta let them know that it doesn't work that way. All these parents we know, kid announces, "Trisha just called. She wants me to come over," the parents act like General Powell just ordered them to march on Baghdad. Okay! Well! Let's change all our plans! You get the dinner, I'll get the car, you cancel the reservations—it's like the boss just walked into the office and caught everybody updating their Facebook page and watching porn. Everybody's scrambling because the kid announced a thought.

You know what? Kids have lots of thoughts.

Parents should have a few of their own. And if one of those happens to involve telling their kid not to interrupt when grown-ups are talking, all the better.

Good thing there are no kids reading this book right now, or I'm sure one of them would have figured out how to interrupt already.

6. THE HEAVY-DUTY PARENT.

This is a thing that I see a lot in New York. It's mostly with parents of little ones, like one- and two-year-olds. The parents are walking around with the kid and narrating the entire world for them. Look, look at that doggie, isn't that a nice doggie? Look, there's a tree, don't you love that tree? Look, there's a big fat actor who used to be on *The Sopranos*, and he's glaring at me like he wants to hit me, we never hit, do we? No, we never hit. Right, Mr. Big Fat Actor?

There's this one mom, has to do this in the elevator, every time I'm in there with her. "Let's count the buttons, honey! Can you see the number seven? Which is the seven? Is this the seven? Yes, this is the seven! Very good! You found the seven!"

First of all, she didn't find the seven. You found the goddamn seven, and how the hell is the kid gonna ever learn anything if you praise her for just standing there with her thumb in her mouth staring at you like you're a crazy person, which, not to put too fine a point on it, you are. And second of all, we all know you're doing this for my benefit. You wanna teach your kid to recognize numbers, fine. Wait until you're in your own apartment, and have her pick the lottery numbers for you, because she's gonna need the money to pay for therapy in about ten years because her mother was just a goddamn annoying nut job. Shut up already for two minutes.

7. NOT SO LOUD.

Now, the flip side of parents who can't stop teaching their kids in public are the parents who can't stop yelling at their kids in public. I think I've established by now that I am not the quietest parent on the PTA e-mail list. That I am not above raising my voice a few decibels if the situation calls for it, or, for that matter, if the situation doesn't actually call for it but I feel it would be useful, or if I just need to let off a little steam because you're driving me nuts right in this very moment. But I will say this: When I yell at my kids, I do it in private. That's something between them and me.

There's this one woman on my block. She's yelling at her kids all the time. Two cutest little girls you ever saw, and she's constantly yelling at them. I mean constantly. Lady is a whack job. Talk about needing to start saving now for the kids' therapy later—you look at the look on these kids' faces when the mom is yelling at them, it would break your heart.

Look, truth of the matter is, I don't really yell at my kids if I don't have to. But I will question them pretty strongly. It's more a matter of being a good protector who asks the right question, rather than being the warden who locks them up later. Hey, what are you doing? Why are you doing this? What did I say? Didn't I tell you earlier? Why are you doing this if I told you not to?

But like I said, that's between us. That's in private. Not in public. I don't need to hear you yell at your kids. I got my own problems.

8. MORE PARENTS WHO NEED TO BE SLAPPED.

What, you thought I was finished? I'm just getting started. Here are some more parents who need to be slapped:

- Parents who make their four-year-old take tennis lessons because it fills the time between the kid's cello practice and his yoga class.

- Parents who name their kids "Sparrow," "Apple," or "Denim" and then wonder why the kids need a shrink.

- Parents who get their kids PlayStation, Xbox, Wii, and every iPad app there is, and then get mad when their kids never play outside.

- People who don't have kids telling me how to raise mine.

- Douche bag dads who wear those Bluetooth earpieces everywhere. (It's got nothing to do with being a dad. It just annoys the hell out of me.)

- Parents who let their four-year-old kid talk at the top of his voice in the airplane lounge—without telling him to take it down a notch. (I'm sitting in the airplane lounge right now watching this happen right in front of me. I don't know whether to stuff the doughnut I'm eating in my ears or in the kid's mouth.)

- Dads with trophy wives who treat their kids from their first marriage like stool samples.

- Dads who brag nonstop about their kids even though they only get to see them every other weekend.

9. VAMPIRE TEENAGERS.

Everybody wants to know why teenagers are so into vampire movies these days. I think there's an easy explanation.

It's because, left to their own devices, they'd become vampires themselves.

I don't mean the bloodsucking thing. Although, given what makes up most kids' diets these days, it would probably improve their nutrition. I'm talking about kids who keep their shades closed and sleep until four in the afternoon.

And, more important, I'm talking about the parents who let them.

I know a lot of parents say, well, you know teenagers. They need to sleep a lot because they're growing. You know what?

Let them get up at a decent hour and grow a little less. Who needs such tall kids anyway? Let the sun shine in.

I don't think it's healthy for kids to sit around in the dark, or sleep until the middle of the afternoon, and then wander around in their pajamas until dinnertime. This doesn't happen in my house. I think it makes you lazy. It makes your mind lazy. It makes your body lazy. And there's no reason for it.

I don't mind if the kid wants to sleep an extra hour or two on the weekends, but you know what? Sometime on the near side of ten o'clock, the kid needs to open a shade, open a window, get cleaned up, get dressed, make the bed. I don't care what my kids do once they're up—watch TV, for all I care— but don't lie there in the dark. Act like a live person. This is not a bad habit to get into. Acting like a live person comes in very handy out in the real world. You should make your kids try it.

10. SOME MORE THINGS THAT PISS ME OFF, JUST IN CASE YOU WERE WONDERING.

- Guys who need spandex pants to ride a bicycle.

- People who post photos of newborns—they all look like Edward G. Robinson to me, so why not just post a photo of him?

- Cartoons where the characters "share" and "talk out their problems" rather than drop anvils or grand pianos on each other's heads.

- Anyone who uses the term "BFF." You can go BFF yourself.

- Kids from the suburbs who talk and dress like they were born in the ghetto. Let them go into the hood and see how long they last.

- Women who think they're a MILF when they're really a BARF.

Yeah, I know. Those are not all about parents. I just had to get these off my chest. I feel better now.

11. SO-CALLED REALITY TV.

Now, when I say I don't care if my kids watch TV, there's one exception. Not to put too fine a point on it, but I think reality television could very well be the downfall of this country.

Well, that and the designated hitter rule. But that's a whole 'nother story.

Take MTV for example. Remember when MTV used to play music videos, and there was all this outrage from people like Tipper Gore because the lyrics of the songs were so suggestive, and the videos were even more so? Man, that was like putting skirts around the legs of pianos, compared to what goes on MTV today.

A couple years back, they start making these shows, one more disgusting than the next. *The Real World* got raunchier and raunchier. *Teen Mom*—don't even get me started. And then *Skins*—it's like porn for teenagers. Here's the plot: Let's do drugs and have sex. No, let's do sex and have drugs. No, let's do some different drugs and do sex with some other people. Who the hell programs this shit? The network defended *Skins* because it was on at ten p.m. Good move. Like teenagers aren't up that late, and like nobody knows how to program a DVR to record this crap (I mean, I don't know how to program a DVR to record anything. I'm lucky if I turn on the coffee machine and it doesn't make orange juice. But I'm just saying).

The trouble is, kids watch this and they think it's normal behavior. That actual people behave this way in the actual world. I mean, I'm sure they do, but I'm talking about outside of a crack house.

The trouble is, MTV and the rest of them—E! and VH1 are pretty bad with this shit, too, but it's really all across the spectrum—they make celebrities out of people like Paris Hilton and Lindsay Lohan and Kim Kardashian just for being trashy, disgusting skanks. Like it's something to aspire to.

Jersey Shore—that doesn't just make Italians look bad, it makes the whole human race look bad. It's acceptable to punch people, punch girls, get drunk, puke, fuck. Kids watch that and think that's okay. If they do it on TV and we watch it, it must be okay. *Pimp My Ride.* Really? Are you kidding me? Pimping? You have kids talking about pimps and hoes like it's a part of normal conversation. I mean, pimping? One of the most despicable human beings that could ever fucking walk the face of the earth is a pimp who preys on young girls. Are you kidding me?

I've got nothing against rap music. Some of these guys are very talented. But this whole business of calling women bitches and hoes—this is just wrong. And you have some kid listening to this and thinking that's how the world is supposed to be.

Mob Wives, over on VH1. There's another one. How far does this go? What's next? We'll start murdering people in prime time? Where does this end?

Some people argue that they're showing this stuff to put it up as a negative stereotype.

Some people are full of shit.

They're not showing this stuff to make it look negative. They're showing it to sell advertising and make money. And when the so-called stars of these shows hit it big, and the talk show hosts suck up to them to get them on the talk shows, to boost their ratings, you think those talk show hosts are gonna say, what's the matter with you, you sick fuck? Why are you behaving like this on national television? No, of course not, because they'll never get them on the show again, or any other reality TV personalities either once the word gets out.

So they have them on, and ask them tough questions like, "Did you ever expect that you would become this famous?"—I swear to God, I heard this one talk show host fawning over Snookie, whoever the hell she is, the poster girl for demented behavior. How can you fawn over these degenerates? Because that's the turning point right there. They can act however they're gonna act, and MTV can put them on the air all they want, but when they go out in the real world and the first question anyone asks isn't, "What the hell is the matter with you? Did they drop you on your head as a baby, or what?"— well, then, that's the ball game. Because now my kid is watching this, and wondering, is this normal behavior, and there's some idiot talk show host treating the Kardashians or Snookie or whoever like they're not disgusting, vile skanks, and my kid is gonna think, Oh, well, I guess that's okay, then.

Only, not my kids. Because they're not watching this shit.

I catch them watching it, the first thing I do, I start questioning them. I caught Bria watching *Keeping Up with the Kardashians* one night. I said, really? This is what you think is good television? You're proud of yourself that you've chosen this as the way to spend your time? This is a woman who's famous for supposedly getting pissed on in a sex tape, and this is what you want to watch? You're not smarter than that? Bruce Jenner, one of the greatest athletes in U.S. history, allowing himself to look like a freak and a fool on national television, this is worth your time?

All I can see on these shows is stupid people doing stupid things. And I'm afraid it might be catching. Venereal diseases are transmitted through sex; I think there's some other disease that's transmitted by watching people who only think about sex, and I'll be damned if my kids are going to catch it.

Look, I'm not the smartest guy in the world. I'm no intellect. But when I talk to an adult and they tell me, "I watch the *Real Housewives*," "I watch *The Kardashians*," "It's my guilty pleasure," you know what? Guilty or not, you take pleasure in that, you drop a notch in my book. And in most people's books, you know that? And I'm just gonna make sure my kids know that.

Now, I gotta say, I know people might ask, where does a guy who was on *The Sopranos* come off talking about bad behavior on television?

Look, I think there's a huge difference between fiction and so-called reality television. *The Sopranos* was one of the best shows ever on television. But it wasn't putting Tony Soprano up as a role model. Tony Soprano wasn't on the cover of *People* magazine—James Gandolfini might be, but that's the difference. Yes, there's a lot of violence in *The Sopranos*. There's a lot of violence in every mob movie. But that's the point—they're mobsters. Gangsters. Outlaws. They're not supposed to be normal human beings. Look, I grew up around real mob guys, and of course their priorities are totally warped—it's not okay to speak back to your mother, but it's okay to chop some guy's head off and stuff him in the trunk of the car? The point of *The Sopranos* was not to say, yes, it's OK to whack a guy's head off. But the point of *Jersey Shore* seems to be, it's okay to get drunk, throw up, fall down, get in the hot tub, and fuck a guy you met ten minutes ago.

And by the way, I didn't let my kids watch *The Sopranos*, either.

But there is one point I do wanna bring up about *The Sopranos*. Tony cursed around his kids, a lot. That's one thing I don't do. I try not to, anyway. And I don't let them curse in front of me. I don't think I've ever heard my little daughter curse, anyway. (Except one time, I remember, she was about three years old, and she's sitting on the rug, and I guess I must have said something I shouldn't have in front of her, because I'm talking to Laura, and Bria looks up from her doll that she's playing with and says, "That's bullshit, Da-da." Well, you don't want to laugh, because you don't want to encourage it—but let's face it, coming out of a three-year-old, "That's bullshit, Da-da" is about the funniest sentence in the world.)

But really, as she got older, my little one never cursed. My big one, maybe a couple of times. But I laid into her good when I heard it. See, you're not gonna do that. You're gonna be a lady. I see a lot of parents who think it's cool to curse in front of their kids, or let the kids curse in front of them. You know what? You curse in front of your friends, I can't stop that. But I can be the one person in your life who will be honest enough to tell you that when you do it, you sound like a skank. There are some people in your life who never curse, and you know what? People respect that. I'm never gonna be that fucking person. But I can help you be that person. You're smarter than that. You're better than that. Me, I grew up on the street, and this is how I am. You, you grew up in a better life, this is how you are. Be that person. Don't be someone who thinks she needs to sound trashy or act trashy or dress trashy to get somebody's attention. That kind of attention, you don't need.

And it goes beyond that. I just don't happen to like hearing young girls curse. Do I curse? Yes. So, you think it's hypocritical for me to say I don't like to hear young girls curse?

Go fuck yourself.

The point is, hearing young girls curse makes me uncomfortable, and in my house I get to feel comfortable. That's a very simple idea that a lot of parents just forget about. It's not a bad thing for kids to have to live up to your expectations in this way.

Not in every way. You want them to live up to your expectations that they get straight As, play the violin perfectly, and get voted class president? Okay, now you're driving them crazy. But you want them to live up to your expectations that they clean their room, open their shades, talk in a polite tone of voice, and don't curse? This will not kill them. These are good habits for them to get into.

Have I made myself fucking clear?

ACKNOWLEDGMENTS

There are a lot of people who helped me get from the idea of writing a book about being a dad to actually getting the thing done. I have to thank Stacy Creamer and Matthew Benjamin, at Touchstone, for their faith in me and for letting me take a shot at this; and my man Mike Harriot for all his help along the way.

I also have to thank the dads: Michael Imperioli, Tim Van Patten, Anson Williams, Felix Rappaport, William Arnone, Hugh Fink, Charles Tremayne, Joe Piscopo, Mitch Modell, Lon Bronson, and all the other fathers who had the balls to tell me what really goes on in their house. We changed the names of a bunch of dads, mostly to save their daughters any more embarrassment than they've already suffered—but I still wanna thank those dads for sharing their stories with me. A special thanks to Joe Medeiros, not just for sharing the stories of his kids, but for really helping me get this book rolling and for contributing lots of funny ideas. Joe, you always make me laugh. And a special thanks to Phil Lerman, who's not only a funny guy but a really good guy and a great father. It was a pleasure to work with you.

There's lots of other people who've helped me out along the way: Thanks to Robby Kass, Bill Veloric, Henry S. Schleiff, Lisa Perkins, Roger Haber, Val Baugh, Lorraine Schirripa, Brenda Hampton, Joe Scarpinito, Diane Costello, Dan Schoenberg, Barry Watkins, Mike Severino, Joe Demeo, Charles Najjar, Sal Bugliore,

Bob Fiandra, Robyn Snyder, Jimmy Raya, Drew Nieporent, Bob Getman, Mike Sammaciccia, Charles Fleming, Ray Favero, Frank DeCarlo, Jimmy Vivino, Rory Rosegarten, Dan Bodansky, Tom Leonardis, Jeff Sussman, Meredith Kennedy, Bill Glasser, Mary Stoffel, Bobby and Carly, and the folks down at Harry's Italian. And I know I probably left out some people—my memory ain't what it used to be—but you know who you are and you know you have my gratitude.

And, of course, most of all, thanks to Laura, Bria, and Ciara for reminding me, every day, what it's really all about. I'm nothing without you.